BLACK HISTORY 2012
Discovery & Reflection

with images from the LIBRARY OF CONGRESS

Pomegranate

Catalog No. W086

Published by Pomegranate Communications, Inc.
Box 808022, Petaluma CA 94975

Available in the UK and mainland Europe from Pomegranate Europe Ltd.
Unit 1, Heathcote Business Centre, Hurlbutt Road, Warwick, Warwickshire CV34 6TD, UK

Images courtesy Library of Congress, unless otherwise specified. All rights reserved.
Text © 2011 IOKTS Productions • www.iokts.com

Pomegranate also publishes the calendars *A Journey into 366 Days of Black History, African American Art, Romare Bearden,* and a wide variety of other 2012 calendars in wall, mini wall, coloring, engagement, postcard, specialty, and 366-day tear-off formats. Our extensive line of paper gift products and books can be found at fine retailers throughout the world and online. For more information or to place an order, please contact Pomegranate Communications, Inc., 800 227 1428, www.pomegranate.com.

The Library of Congress, often called "the nation's memory," houses some 130 million items from around the world. Among these are the rich and varied collections of the Prints and Photographs Division, from which most of the photographs in this calendar are drawn. Duplicates of images appearing in this calendar that are accompanied by Library of Congress negative numbers (e.g., LC-USZ62-XXXX) may be ordered from the Library of Congress, Duplication Services, Washington, DC 20540-4570; telephone (202) 707-5640; fax (202) 707-1771.

Front cover:
Lou Stovall (American, b. 1937)
Sea to Shining Sea, 2008
Silkscreen, 50.7 x 50.7 cm (20 x 20 in.)
Prints and Photographs Division, LC-DIG-ds-00043

Designed by Stephanie Odeh

Dates in color indicate US federal holidays.
Dates listed for all astronomical events in this calendar are based on Coordinated Universal Time (UTC),
the worldwide system of civil timekeeping. UTC is essentially equivalent to Greenwich Mean Time.
Moon phases and American, Canadian, and UK holidays are noted.
Dates of Islamic holidays are based on promulgations of the Fiqh Council of North America.

 NEW MOON FIRST QUARTER FULL MOON LAST QUARTER

Welcome to a brand-new *Black History* experience! In these pages you'll find a wealth of information, easy-to-reference monthly calendar grids, and lots of room for noting your own thoughts.

Forty-eight artworks and photographs from the Library of Congress, accompanied by illuminating text, feature notable individuals in the areas of politics, science, the arts, education, activism, sports, and civil rights. For every day of the year, there is at least one historical entry detailing a notable event. And, during each month, you'll have the opportunity to reflect on what you've discovered and how it might inspire your future.

IOKTS Productions ("I Only Know the Story") is dedicated to the research of documented history for the purpose of exhibiting the contributions of black people from all cultures, races, and geographic locations. Through this work we strive to promote awareness, knowledge, and understanding among all people while furthering pride, dignity, and inspiration in those who identify directly with this heritage.

We hope you enjoy *Black History 2012: Discovery & Reflection,* and we welcome your feedback. E-mail us at ioktspro@verizon.net or contact:

Mr. G. Theodore Catherine
IOKTS Productions
P.O. Box 11275
Takoma Park, MD 20913
(301) 270-1920

JANUARY

SUNDAY	MONDAY	TUESDAY	WEDNESDAY	THURSDAY	FRIDAY	SATURDAY
◑ 1	2	3	4	5	6	7
8	○ 9	10	11	12	13	14
15	◑ 16	17	18	19	20	21
22	● 23	24	25	26	27	28
29	30	◑ 31				

JAN 1   NEW YEAR'S DAY

JAN 2   NEW YEAR'S DAY HOLIDAY
           BANK HOLIDAY (CANADA, UK)

JAN 3   BANK HOLIDAY (SCOTLAND)

JAN 16   MARTIN LUTHER KING JR. DAY

JAN 23   LUNAR NEW YEAR

GEORGE E. C. HAYES, THURGOOD MARSHALL, JAMES M. NABRIT JR. (LEFT TO RIGHT) • CIVIL RIGHTS ATTORNEYS

Pictured here are Thurgood Marshall (1908–1993), the pioneering NAACP attorney who spearheaded that organization's civil rights cases—and who, most notably, won the United States Supreme Court case *Brown v. Board of Education* in 1954—and his legal team, George E. C. Hayes (1894–1968) and James M. Nabrit Jr. (1900–1997). They are congratulating one another after the Court's landmark decision that school segregation was unconstitutional. Marshall was instrumental in arguing for equal rights in the most critical issues of his time, and he was successful in a large percentage of those cases. In 1967 President Lyndon Johnson appointed him to the Supreme Court; Marshall was the first African American to hold that position.

George E. C. Hayes became the first African American to serve on the District of Columbia Public Utilities Commission. James M. Nabrit Jr. taught the first formal civil rights law course at an American law school. He later became dean of the School of Law at Howard University, and he served as the university's president from 1960 to 1969.

Photographer unknown
Prints and Photographs Division, LC-USZ62-111236

NORA HOLT • SINGER, COMPOSER, MUSIC CRITIC

Nora Douglas Holt (1885–1974) was a gifted musician, composer, writer, and educator who excelled in whatever she attempted. A versatile woman described as "physically stunning," Holt made her mark during the Harlem Renaissance period. Born Lena Douglas in Kansas City, Kansas, she graduated as valedictorian from Western University and then attended Chicago Musical College, where she became the first African American woman to earn a master's degree in the United States. She was a music critic for the *Chicago Defender* and New York's *Amsterdam News,* publisher and editor of *Music and Poetry,* cofounder and vice president of the National Association of Negro Musicians, and composer of some two hundred works. Later she taught music in Los Angeles public schools and hosted radio programs featuring African American classical artists.

Holt traveled in Europe and Asia, performing in nightclubs and at private parties, and associated with leading figures of the Harlem Renaissance. She maintained a close lifelong friendship with the writer and photographer Carl Van Vechten, whose novels included characters based on Holt.

Photograph by Carl Van Vechten
Prints and Photographs Division, LC-USZ62-114531

JANUARY

1

Kwanzaa ends: Imani (Faith). *To believe with all our hearts in our people, our parents, our teachers, our leaders, and the righteousness and victory of our struggle.*

1804 Haiti declares its independence.

1937 Lou Stovall, artist and master printmaker, is born in Athens, GA.

2

1898 Sadie Tanner Mossell Alexander, first African American to earn a PhD in economics, is born in Philadelphia, PA.

1915 John Hope Franklin, historian, educator, and author of *From Slavery to Freedom: A History of Negro Americans*, is born in Rentiesville, OK.

3

1621 William Tucker is the first known child of Africans to be born in America.

1956 Colored Methodist Church, established in 1870, officially changes its name to Christian Methodist Episcopal Church.

4

1787 Prince Hall, founder of the first black Masonic lodge, and others petition the Massachusetts legislature for funds to return to Africa, the first recorded effort by blacks to do so.

1920 Andrew "Rube" Foster organizes the first black baseball league, the Negro National League.

5

1911 Kappa Alpha Psi fraternity is chartered as a national organization.

1931 Alvin Ailey, dancer and founder of his eponymous company, is born in Rogers, TX.

6

1993 Jazz trumpeter John Birks "Dizzy" Gillespie dies in Englewood, NJ.

1996 Recycling Black Dollars, an organization of black businesses, campaigns for "Change Bank Day" to benefit black-owned financial institutions.

7

1891 Folklorist and novelist Zora Neale Hurston is born in Notasulga, AL.

1997 Former South African president Pieter W. Botha is prosecuted for refusing to appear before the nation's truth commission.

8

1922 Col. Charles Young, first African American to achieve that rank in the US Army, dies in Lagos, Nigeria.

9

1866 Fisk University is founded in Nashville, TN.

1906 Renowned poet and writer Paul Laurence Dunbar dies in Dayton, OH.

1914 Phi Beta Sigma fraternity is founded at Howard University.

10

1864 George Washington Carver, scientist and inventor, is born in Diamond Grove, MO.

1924 Drummer Max Roach, influential in the development of modern jazz, is born in New Land, NC.

JANUARY

11

1940 Benjamin O. Davis Sr. becomes the US Army's first black general.

12

1890 Mordecai W. Johnson, first black president of Howard University (a position he will hold for 34 years), is born in Paris, TN. He goes on to receive the NAACP's Spingarn Medal in 1929.
1996 Pioneering sports journalist Sam Skinner dies in Burlingame, CA.
2010 A 7.0 magnitude earthquake devastates the island nation of Haiti.

13

1913 Delta Sigma Theta sorority is founded at Howard University.

14

1916 Author John Oliver Killens is born in Macon, GA.
1940 Julian Bond, civil rights leader and Georgia state senator, is born in Nashville, TN.

15

1908 Alpha Kappa Alpha sorority is founded at Howard University by Ethel Hedgeman Lyle.

16

1920 Zeta Phi Beta sorority is founded at Howard University.
1974 Noted singer-composer Leon Bukasa of Zaire dies.

17

1882 Lewis H. Latimer is granted a patent for the process of manufacturing carbon filaments for lightbulbs.
1942 Muhammad Ali, heavyweight boxing champion, is born in Louisville, KY.

18

1856 Daniel Hale Williams, first physician to perform open-heart surgery and founder of Provident Hospital in Chicago, IL, is born in Hollidaysburg, PA.

19

1887 Clementine Hunter, noted African American painter, is born in Natchitoches, LA.
1918 John H. Johnson, editor and publisher of *Ebony* and *Jet* magazines, is born in Arkansas City, AR.

20

1974 Stevie Wonder plays a gig at Rainbow Theatre, London, after recovering from a nearly fatal car accident five months earlier.
2009 Barack Obama, inaugurated as the 44th president of the United States, becomes the country's first African American president.

ROBERT HAYDEN • POET, ESSAYIST, EDUCATOR

Born in Detroit, Robert Hayden (1913–1980) grew up in a poor neighborhood under difficult circumstances. Life in his foster home was strained and conflicted, and his severe nearsightedness and small stature attracted ridicule from his peers. Hayden found solace in poetry and literature. He attended Detroit City College (Wayne State University) on a scholarship and then was employed by the federal Works Progress Administration, researching black history and folklore. Later he wrote for the *Michigan Chronicle*, married, and published his first book of poetry.

During his graduate work in English literature at the University of Michigan, Hayden studied poetry with W. H. Auden, who became a significant influence. After earning his master's degree, Hayden taught at Fisk University and then the University of Michigan, devoting his spare time to writing. His works became internationally known. However, even though he wrote about black subjects, he was criticized for not identifying himself as a "Negro" poet. Hayden took the position that he was an American poet who happened to be black. He was a visionary who transcended racial limitations.

In 1966 Hayden was named Poet Laureate of Senegal; in 1975 he was elected to the Academy of American Poets; and in 1976 he became the first African American Consultant in Poetry to the Library of Congress, the position now known as United States Poet Laureate.

Photograph by Timothy D. Franklin

Prints and Photographs Division, LC-USZ62-110604

THE DREAM OF NAT TURNER • PAINTING BY BERNARDA BRYSON

This painting by Bernarda Bryson (American, 1903–2004) depicts the revolutionary Nat Turner dreaming about the insurrection he would ultimately carry out. Turner (1800–1831) was a highly intelligent slave in Southampton County, Virginia. Unlike most slaves, Turner could read, and he often read Bible stories to other slaves, which earned him the nickname "the Prophet." A very spiritual man, he was known to have visions that he thought were messages from God. Although he was well liked by the whites in his town, many suspected he should be watched carefully.

Always looking for a sign from God, Turner firmly believed that he was chosen to lead a rebellion that would free the slaves. He planned this uprising, enlisting other slaves, and on August 21, 1831, he and his followers killed fifty-six whites in an attempt to free all the slaves. For his actions he was caught and executed. His lawyer later published an account of the revolt in *The Confessions of Nat Turner.*

Among the many works for which painter and lithographer Bernarda Bryson is known are the children's books she wrote and illustrated and the murals she painted with her future husband, Ben Shahn. Bryson's maternal grandfather's home was a stop on the Underground Railroad.

Bernarda Bryson (American, 1903–2004)
The Dream of Nat Turner, 1935
Ink and watercolor on paper
Prints and Photographs Division, LC-DIG-ppmsca-06780

JANUARY

21   **1993**   Congressman Mike Espy of Mississippi is confirmed as secretary of agriculture.

22   **1906**   Pioneering aviator Willa Brown-Chappell is born in Glasgow, KY.
       1935   Singer Sam Cooke, best known for "You Send Me" and "Twisting the Night Away," is born in Chicago, IL.

23   **1941**   Richard Wright is awarded the NAACP's Spingarn Medal.
       1964   The 24th Amendment is ratified, abolishing the poll tax.

24   **1985**   Tom Bradley, four-term mayor of Los Angeles, receives the NAACP's Spingarn Medal for public service.

25   **1890**   The National Afro-American League, a pioneering black protest organization, is founded in Chicago, IL.
       1966   Constance Baker Motley becomes the first African American woman to be appointed to a federal judgeship.

26   **1927**   Singer, dancer, and actor Eartha Mae Kitt is born in Columbia, SC.
       1944   Angela Yvonne Davis, political activist and educator, is born in Birmingham, AL.

27   **1972**   Gospel music legend Mahalia Jackson dies in Evergreen Park, IL.

28   **1944**   Matthew Henson receives a joint medal from Congress as codiscoverer of the North Pole.

29   **1872**   Francis L. Cardoza is elected South Carolina state treasurer.
       1926   Violette Neatley Anderson becomes the first African American woman admitted to practice before the US Supreme Court.

30   **1844**   Richard Theodore Greener becomes the first African American to graduate from Harvard University.

31   **1919**   Jackie Robinson, first African American to play in major league baseball, is born in Cairo, GA.
       2006   Coretta Scott King dies in Mexico.
       2009   In Molo, Kenya, at least 113 people are killed and over 200 injured when an oil spill is ignited.

JANUARY REFLECTIONS

This month I was inspired by:

I'd like to know more about:

The people featured this month and the historical entries brought up these memories:

Next month I would like to:

JANUARY REFLECTIONS

RANDOM THOUGHTS

BOOKS TO READ

MUSIC TO HEAR

PERFORMANCES TO SEE

FEBRUARY

			1	2	3	4
5	6	○ 7	8	9	10	11
12	13	◑ 14	15	16	17	18
19	20	● 21	22	23	24	25
26	27	28	29			

FEB   7   INDEPENDENCE DAY (GRENADA)

FEB   14   VALENTINE'S DAY

FEB   18   NATIONAL INDEPENDENCE DAY (GAMBIA)

FEB   20   PRESIDENTS' DAY

FEB   21   MARDI GRAS

FEB   22   ASH WEDNESDAY

FEB   23   REPUBLIC DAY (GUYANA)

FEB   27   INDEPENDENCE DAY (DOMINICAN REPUBLIC)

NORMAL CLASS AT ROGER WILLIAMS UNIVERSITY

Roger Williams University in Nashville, Tennessee, was a historically black university founded in 1866 to educate newly freed slaves. (It had no connection with the present-day university of the same name in Rhode Island.) The school began in 1864 as a Baptist college, training African American preachers; in 1866 it expanded its curriculum and was renamed the Nashville Normal and Theological Institute. The Institute purchased land near Vanderbilt University in 1874 and built a new campus there, and in 1883 it incorporated as Roger Williams University, with African Americans holding faculty positions and serving on the board of trustees. The curriculum was further expanded in 1886 to include a master's degree program.

This photograph was taken in 1899, six years before mysterious fires destroyed the school's buildings. Students were transferred to Atlanta Baptist College (Morehouse University); eventually the Nashville campus was closed and the university merged with LeMoyne-Owen College in Memphis.

Photographer unknown
Prints and Photographs Division, LC-USZ62-126751

803RD PIONEER INFANTRY BAND

When the US armed services send troops to war, efforts are always made to provide them with entertainment. Groups such as the USO, celebrity-sponsored programs, and military bands help lift the morale of soldiers who are away from home and experiencing the hardships of war.

This photograph shows the African American members of the 803rd Pioneer Infantry Band on the USS *Philippine* as they embarked on a voyage back home from Brest, a city in northwestern France, in July 1919. These musicians, who were also soldiers prepared for battle, brought great joy to the Allied troops and citizens of the war theater.

The 803rd helped introduce "American classical music"—also known as jazz—to French and American troops. During this period it was common for African American soldiers to receive better treatment in Europe than at home, where discrimination still was law. In France, African American troops were welcomed and treated with respect. In gratitude, the 803rd Infantry Band worked hard to raise the spirits of the fighting soldiers by playing great music.

803rd Pioneer Infantry Battalion on the U.S.S. Philippine *from Brest Harbor, France, July 18, 1919. No. 16, 803rd Pioneer Infantry Band*
Photographer unknown
Prints and Photographs Division, LC-DIG-ppmsca-11434

FEBRUARY

1

1865 John S. Rock becomes the first black attorney to practice before the US Supreme Court.
1902 Prolific poet Langston Hughes is born in Joplin, MO.

2

1915 Biologist Ernest E. Just receives the Spingarn Medal for his pioneering research in fertilization and cell division.

3

1947 Percival Prattis, of *Our World in New York City*, becomes the first black news correspondent admitted to the House and Senate press galleries in Washington, DC.
1948 Portraitist and illustrator Laura Wheeler Waring dies in Philadelphia.

4

1913 Rosa Parks, initiator of the Montgomery bus boycott, is born in Tuskegee, AL.
1969 The Popular Liberation Movement of Angola begins armed struggle against the country's colonial Portuguese government.

5

1934 Hank Aaron, a major league baseball home run king, is born in Mobile, AL.
1994 White supremacist Byron De La Beckwith is convicted of the murder of Medgar Evers, more than 30 years after Evers was ambushed and shot in the back.

6

1993 Arthur Ashe, tennis player, humanitarian, and activist, dies in New York City.

7

1926 Negro History Week, originated by Carter G. Woodson, is observed for the first time.

8

1925 Marcus Garvey enters federal prison in Atlanta, GA.
1944 Harry S. McAlphin of Atlanta's *Daily World* becomes the first black journalist accredited to attend White House press conferences.

9

1944 Alice Walker, Pulitzer Prize–winning author, is born in Eatonton, GA.

10

1780 Capt. Paul Cuffee and six other black residents of Massachusetts petition the state legislature for the right to vote.
1869 Nat Love, former slave from Tennessee, goes west to make his fortune. He becomes known as Deadwood Dick, one of the most famous cowboys, black or white, in history.

FEBRUARY

11
1990 Nelson Mandela is released from a South African prison after 27 years as a political prisoner.
2008 Morgan Tsvangirai is sworn in as prime minister of Zimbabwe following a power-sharing deal with President Robert Mugabe.

12
1896 Isaac Burns Murphy, one of the greatest jockeys of all time, dies in Lexington, KY.

13
1907 Wendell P. Dabney establishes *The Union*, a Cincinnati paper whose motto is "For no people can become great without being united, for in union, there is strength."
1970 Joseph L. Searles becomes the first black member of the New York Stock Exchange.

14
1817 Frederick Douglass, "the Great Emancipator," is born in Talbot County, MD.
1867 Morehouse College is founded in Augusta, GA; it later moves to Atlanta.

15
1961 US activists and African nationalists disrupt UN sessions to protest the slaying of Congo premier Patrice Lumumba.

16
1826 *The Liberia Herald*, first newspaper printed in Africa, is published by C. L. Force of Boston, MA.
1923 Bessie Smith makes her first recording, "Down-Hearted Blues," which sells 800,000 copies for Columbia Records.

17
1938 Mary Frances Berry, first woman to serve as chancellor of a major research university (University of Colorado), is born in Nashville, TN.
1982 Pianist Thelonious Monk, a founding father of modern jazz, dies from a massive stroke in Weehawken, NJ.

18
1688 Quakers of Germantown, PA, adopt the first formal antislavery resolution in American history.

19
1919 W. E. B. Du Bois organizes the second Pan-African Congress in Paris.

20
1927 Sidney Poitier, first African American to win an Academy Award in a starring role, is born in Miami, FL.
1929 Wallace Thurman's play *Harlem* begins a successful run on Broadway.

SOLDIER GUARDING TWELVE-POUNDER NAPOLEONS

The twelve-pounder Napoleon cannon was an essential element of Civil War weaponry and was the most popular cannon used by both Union and Confederate troops. This field artillery weapon was developed in France in 1853 and named after Napoleon III of France. "Twelve-pounder" refers to the gun's ability to fire a twelve-pound solid ball from its long barrel. The original twelve-pounder was a cumbersome, heavy weapon that required a team of eight horses to maneuver it from place to place. The Napoleon model shown here (possibly model 1857) was lighter and required only six horses.

In this 1865 photograph taken in City Point, Virginia, an African American soldier guards an arsenal of twelve-pounder Napoleons. Ironically, African American soldiers were not always trusted to bear arms, yet this black soldier is guarding an array of the most powerful weapons on the Civil War battlefield.

Photographer unknown
Prints and Photographs Division, LC-DIG-cwpb-01982

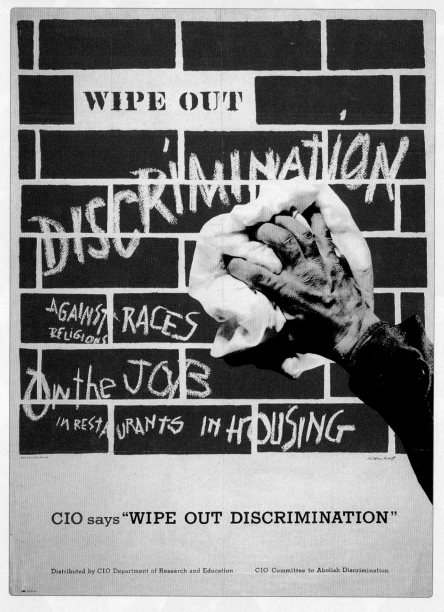

WIPE OUT DISCRIMINATION · POSTER BY MILTON ACKOFF

In this 1949 *Wipe Out Discrimination* poster by artist Milton Ackoff, the Congress of Industrial Organizations (CIO), a federation of labor unions, was attempting to show support of the civil rights movement. In 1955 the CIO merged with the American Federation of Labor, becoming the AFL-CIO, the largest federation of unions in the United States.

Milton Ackoff (American, b. 1915)
Wipe Out Discrimination: CIO Says "Wipe Out Discrimination," 1949
Lithograph, 116.8 x 83.8 cm (46 x 33 in.)
Prints and Photographs Division, LC-USZC4-2766

FEBRUARY

21   **1965**   El-Hajj Malik el-Shabazz (Malcolm X), American black nationalist, is assassinated in New York City.

22   **1841**   Grafton Tyler Brown, one of California's first African American painters, is born in Harrisburg, PA.
1962   Wilt Chamberlain sets an NBA record with 34 attempted free throws.

23   **1972**   Political activist Angela Davis is released from jail.

24   **1966**   Military leaders oust Kwame Nkrumah, president of Ghana, while he is in Beijing on a peace mission to stop the Vietnam War.
2008   Raúl Castro is elected president of Cuba after his brother Fidel resigns.

25   **1978**   Daniel "Chappie" James, first African American four-star general, dies in Colorado Springs, CO.
1991   Adrienne Mitchell becomes the first black woman in the US armed forces to die in combat. She is killed in her military barracks in Saudi Arabia during the Persian Gulf War.

26   **1926**   Theodore "Tiger" Flowers (aka "the Georgia Deacon") defeats Harry Greb in New York City, becoming the first black middleweight champion of the world.
1928   Singer Antoine "Fats" Domino is born in New Orleans, LA.

27   **1872**   Charlotte Ray graduates from Howard University's law school, becoming the first female African American lawyer.

28   **1948**   Sgt. Cornelius F. Adjetey becomes the first martyr for the national independence of Ghana.

29   **1892**   Augusta Savage, sculptor and educator, is born in Green Cove Springs, FL.
1940   Hattie McDaniel becomes the first African American to win an Academy Award, for her role as Mammy in *Gone with the Wind*.

FEBRUARY REFLECTIONS

This month I was inspired by:

I'd like to know more about:

The people featured this month and the historical entries brought up these memories:

Next month I would like to:

FEBRUARY REFLECTIONS

RANDOM THOUGHTS

BOOKS TO READ

MUSIC TO HEAR

PERFORMANCES TO SEE

MARCH

SUNDAY	MONDAY	TUESDAY	WEDNESDAY	THURSDAY	FRIDAY	SATURDAY
				◐ 1	2	3
4	5	6	7	○ 8	9	10
11	12	13	14	◐ 15	16	17
18	19	20	21	● 22	23	24
25	26	27	28	29	◐ 30	31

MAR 3   MARTYR'S DAY (MALAWI)

MAR 6   INDEPENDENCE DAY (GHANA)

MAR 7   PURIM (BEGINS AT SUNSET)

MAR 8   INTERNATIONAL WOMEN'S DAY

MAR 11 DAYLIGHT SAVING TIME BEGINS

MAR 17 ST. PATRICK'S DAY

MAR 18 MOTHERING SUNDAY (UK)

MAR 20 VERNAL EQUINOX 05:14 UTC

MAR 25 SUMMER TIME BEGINS (UK)

A BLACK BELLE, BARBADOS • LITHOGRAPH BY GEORGE HAND WRIGHT

This image of a woman working on the island of Barbados was created by American artist George Hand Wright (1872–1951). Wright, the son of a blacksmith, was born in Fox Chase, Pennsylvania, and studied art at the Pennsylvania Academy of Fine Arts. His illustrations were featured regularly in magazines such as *Century, Scribner's, Harper's,* and *The Saturday Evening Post.* Wright helped found the artistic community in Westport, Connecticut, where he had his studio.

George Hand Wright (American, 1872–1951)
A Black Belle, Barbados, n.d.
Lithograph
Prints and Photographs Division, LC-DIG-ds-00033

MADAME C. J. WALKER • ENTREPRENEUR, PHILANTHROPIST

Madame C. J. Walker (1867–1919), the first self-made female African American millionaire, was very supportive of causes that uplifted the black community. Born Sarah Breedlove, she began her life in poverty, but through hard work and astute marketing and promotion she achieved great success in the beauty, health, and hair care industry. "I am a woman who came from the cotton fields of the South," she said in an address to a business convention in 1912. "From there I was promoted to the washtub ... And from there I promoted myself into the business of manufacturing hair goods and preparations ... I have built my own factory on my own ground." Walker employed thousands of women in the United States and the Caribbean, enabling many to become financially self-sufficient.

Among her numerous philanthropic efforts, Walker contributed to women's scholarships at Tuskegee Institute and Palmer Memorial Institute, and she supported Mary McLeod Bethune's Daytona Normal and Industrial Institute for Negro Girls and Lucy Laney's Haynes Institute in Augusta, Georgia. She contributed to the NAACP, various homes for the aged, and the YWCA in Indianapolis, where her business was headquartered. She was inducted into the National Women's Hall of Fame in Seneca Falls, New York, and cited by Harvard Business School as one of the great American business leaders of the twentieth century. In 1998 she was honored with a US postage stamp as part of the Black Heritage series.

MARCH

1
1871 James Milton Turner is named minister to Liberia, becoming the first black American diplomat accredited to an African country.
1914 Ralph Waldo Ellison, author of the award-winning *Invisible Man*, is born in Oklahoma City.

2
1955 Claudette Colvin refuses to give up her seat on a bus in Montgomery, AL, nine months before Rosa Parks's arrest for the same action sparks the Montgomery bus boycott.

3
1821 Thomas L. Jennings is the first African American to be granted a US patent, for his technique to "dry-scour" clothes.

4
1932 Zensi Miriam Makeba, "Empress of African Song," is born in Prospect Township, South Africa.

5
1770 Crispus Attucks is killed in the Boston Massacre, marking the start of the American Revolution.

6
1857 US Supreme Court rules against citizenship for African Americans in the Dred Scott decision.

7
1539 Estevanico (or Esteban) de Dorantes, a native of Azamoor, Morocco, sets out to explore what is now the southwestern United States.

8
1876 After three years of controversy, the US Senate refuses to seat P. B. S. Pinchback, elected as a Louisiana senator in 1873.
1977 Henry L. Marsh III becomes the first black mayor of Richmond, VA.

9
1914 The "new" Southern University campus opens in Scotlandville, LA, with 9 teachers and 47 students.
1919 Nora Douglas Holt and other black Chicago musicians form the Chicago Musical Association.

10
1845 Women's rights activist Hallie Quinn Brown is born in Pittsburgh, PA.
1963 Actor Jasmine Guy, known as Whitley in the TV series *A Different World*, is born in Boston, MA.

MARCH

11 **1948** Dr. Reginald Weir of New York City wins his first match in the USLTA Tennis Championship Tournament.

12 **1791** Benjamin Banneker and Pierre Charles L'Enfant are commissioned to plan and develop Washington, DC.

13 **1773** Jean-Baptiste Pointe du Sable founds the city of Chicago, IL.
       1943 Frank Dixon becomes the first great black miler in track, winning the Columbian Mile in New York City in a record time of 4 minutes, 9.6 seconds.

14 **1933** Composer, musician, and producer Quincy Delight Jones is born in Chicago, IL.

15 **1947** John Lee becomes the first African American commissioned officer in the US Navy.
       1968 *Life* magazine calls Jimi Hendrix "the most spectacular guitarist in the world."

16 **1827** John Russwurm, first African American college graduate, begins publication of *Freedom's Journal* with Samuel Cornish.
       1995 Mississippi ratifies the 13th Amendment, which abolishes slavery, 130 years after all but three other states approved it.

17 **1865** Aaron Anderson wins the navy's Medal of Honor for his heroic actions aboard USS *Wyandank* during the Civil War.
       1867 Educator Ida Rebecca Cummings is born in Baltimore, MD.

18 **1901** Renowned painter William H. Johnson is born in Florence, SC.
       1992 Singer Donna Summer gets a star on Hollywood's Walk of Fame.

19 **1930** Jazz saxophonist Ornette Coleman is born in Fort Worth, TX.
       1939 Langston Hughes founds the New Negro Theater in Los Angeles. Its first performance is his play *Don't You Want to Be Free?*

20 **1883** Jan Matzeliger receives a patent for the shoe-lasting machine, which launches mass production of shoes.

OSCAR DE PRIEST • US CONGRESSMAN

A trailblazing politician from Chicago, Oscar Stanton De Priest was the city's first black alderman, and he became the first black representative in the US Congress in the twentieth century.

De Priest (1871–1951) was born in Florence, Alabama, to parents who were former slaves. In 1878 the family, like many others, moved to Kansas to escape discrimination and earn a better living; De Priest received his education there. In 1889 he moved to Chicago, where he worked as a house painter and decorator, establishing his own business and a real estate firm, before entering politics. A Republican and a staunch civil rights activist, De Priest served on the Chicago city council, became an alderman, and ultimately was elected to Congress, where he served three terms (1929–1935).

During his time in Congress, De Priest wrote antidiscriminatory legislation and promoted laws against lynching and in favor of equal access to public accommodations. He once requested an official investigation of House cafeteria policies when his secretary, Morris Lewis, was refused service. De Priest (seated) and Lewis (standing) are pictured here in May 1929.

Photographer unknown
Prints and Photographs Division, LC-DIG-npcc-17478

24TH INFANTRY LEAVING SALT LAKE CITY, UTAH

Troops of the all-black 24th Infantry were stationed at Fort Douglas, Utah, a key fort established in 1862, before being deployed to Cuba in 1898 at the beginning of the Spanish-American War. These soldiers served with distinction in the war and were noted for their courageous fighting, particularly in the Battle of San Juan Hill.

When the 24th Infantry arrived in Salt Lake City, the soldiers were met with disdain and vigorous protest from the white citizens. But they eventually won over the townspeople, as demonstrated in this photograph of the soldiers marching down Main Street on April 24, 1898, with citizens lining the streets to bid them farewell.

The noted chaplain Allen Allensworth was part of the 24th Infantry regiment at Fort Douglas. When Allensworth retired from military service in 1906, he was a lieutenant colonel, the first African American to achieve that rank. In 1908, with his wife, Josephine, he founded the prosperous all-black town of Allensworth, California, today the site of Colonel Allensworth State Historic Park.

Photographer unknown

Prints and Photographs Division, LC-USZC4-6174

MARCH

21   **1965**   Martin Luther King Jr. leads thousands of marchers from Selma, heading for Montgomery, AL, to dramatize denial of voting rights to African Americans.

22   **1492**   Alonzo Pietro, explorer, sets sail with Christopher Columbus.

23   **1985**   Patricia Roberts Harris, Cabinet member and ambassador, dies in Washington, DC.

24   **1907**   Nurse and aviator Janet Harmon Bragg is born in Griffin, GA.

25   **1931**   Ida B. Wells-Barnett, journalist, antilynching activist, and founding member of the NAACP, dies in Chicago, IL.

         1939   Toni Cade Bambara, noted fiction writer (*The Sea Birds Are Still Alive; Gorilla, My Love; The Salt Eaters*), is born in New York City.

26   **1886**   Hugh N. Mulzac, the first black to captain an American merchant marine ship (SS *Booker T. Washington*, 1942), is born in the West Indies.

27   **1872**   Musician Cleveland Luca, member of the famous Luca Family Quartet and composer of the Liberian national anthem, dies in Liberia.

         1924   Jazz singer Sarah Vaughan, "the Divine One," is born in Newark, NJ.

28   **1870**   Jonathan S. Wright becomes the first African American state supreme court justice in South Carolina.

29   **1918**   Singer and actor Pearl Bailey is born in Newport News, VA.

         1945   Basketball guard Walt Frazier is born in Atlanta, GA. The future Hall of Famer will lead the New York Knicks to NBA championships in 1970 and 1973.

30   **1948**   Trailblazing fashion model Naomi Sims is born in Oxford, MS.

31   **1871**   Jack Johnson, first African American heavyweight boxing champion, is born in Galveston, TX.

         1988   Toni Morrison wins the Pulitzer Prize for her novel *Beloved*.

MARCH REFLECTIONS

This month I was inspired by:

I'd like to know more about:

The people featured this month and the historical entries brought up these memories:

Next month I would like to:

MARCH REFLECTIONS

RANDOM THOUGHTS

BOOKS TO READ

MUSIC TO HEAR

PERFORMANCES TO SEE

APRIL

SUNDAY	MONDAY	TUESDAY	WEDNESDAY	THURSDAY	FRIDAY	SATURDAY
	1	2	3	4	5	○ 6	7
8	9	10	11	12	◑ 13	14
15	16	17	18	19	20	● 21
22	23	24	25	26	27	28
◐ 29	30					

APR 1 PALM SUNDAY

APR 4 INDEPENDENCE DAY (SENEGAL)

APR 6 GOOD FRIDAY
PASSOVER (BEGINS AT SUNSET)
BANK HOLIDAY (CANADA, UK)

APR 8 EASTER

APR 9 EASTER MONDAY (CANADA, UK
EXCEPT SCOTLAND)
NATIONAL DAY (SIERRA LEONE)

APR 18 INDEPENDENCE DAY (ZIMBABWE)

APR 19 REPUBLIC DAY (SIERRA LEONE)

APR 22 EARTH DAY

AFRIKA HAYES • SINGER, EDUCATOR, ACTOR

Afrika Hayes is the daughter of the great tenor soloist Roland Hayes. Her father was a giant, a superb vocalist, a musical pioneer. His talent, courage, and hard work opened the way for many African American artists who followed him, including Marian Anderson, Leontyne Price, and Paul Robeson. These and other performers rose out of Hayes's shadow to become legends, and so has his daughter, Afrika. She is pictured here in 1964.

Afrika Hayes grew up in an environment saturated with the sound of music. She also benefited from being in the presence of many accomplished individuals who were drawn to the family home by her father's charisma and success. Afrika began playing piano at age three but did not sing professionally until adulthood. Although she was gifted with a fine soprano voice, being the daughter of such an acclaimed singer made her hesitate to express that voice publicly until she was thirty. Along with her successful career as a singer and music educator, Afrika Hayes appeared in the 1990 television documentary *The Musical Legacy of Roland Hayes*.

Photograph by Carl Van Vechten
Prints and Photographs Division, LC-DIG-ds-00042

MIGRANT WORKERS FROM FLORIDA

Recently, controversy has surrounded the topic of migrant workers—"outsiders" brought in from another country or state to work for low wages, performing menial jobs that some say the local workforce will not perform. The migrant workers in the news today are usually Latinos; however, African Americans have also been migrant workers during tough economic times, such as the era of the Great Depression.

When unskilled African Americans sought work, they went where the work existed, despite low wages and harsh conditions. For some it was the only way to survive. This July 1940 photograph from the US Farm Security Administration shows a group of African Americans from Florida stopping near Shawboro, North Carolina, on their way to harvest potatoes in Cranberry, New Jersey.

Photograph by Jack Delano

Prints and Photographs Division, LC-USF34-040841-D

APRIL

1   **1930**   Zauditu, first female monarch of Ethiopia, dies.

2   **1796**   Haitian revolt leader Toussaint L'Ouverture commands French forces at Santo Domingo.

3   **1934**   Richard Mayhew, revolutionary landscape artist, is born in Amityville, NY.
       1984   John Thompson of Georgetown University becomes the first African American coach to win an NCAA basketball tournament.

4   **1968**   Martin Luther King Jr. is assassinated in Memphis, TN.
       2002   Angola's government and UNITA rebels sign a peace treaty ending that country's civil war.

5   **1937**   Colin Powell, first African American to serve as chairman of the Joint Chiefs of Staff and US secretary of state, is born in New York City.

6   **1798**   Noted scout James P. Beckwourth is born in Fredericksburg, VA. He discovered the pass in the Sierra Nevada that bears his name.
       1905   W. Warrick Cardozo, physician and pioneering researcher in sickle cell anemia, is born in Washington, DC.

7   **1867**   Johnson C. Smith University is founded in Charlotte, NC.
       1915   Jazz and blues legend Billie Holiday is born in East Baltimore, MD.

8   **1974**   Hank Aaron breaks Babe Ruth's major league record with 715 career home runs.
       1990   Percy Julian and George Washington Carver are the first black inventors admitted into the National Inventors Hall of Fame.

9   **1898**   Actor and singer Paul Robeson is born in Princeton, NJ.
       1950   Juanita Hall is the first black to win a Tony Award, for her portrayal of Bloody Mary in *South Pacific*.

10   **1943**   Arthur Ashe, first African American to win the men's singles title at both the US Open and Wimbledon, is born in Richmond, VA.

APRIL

11

1996 Forty-three African nations sign the African Nuclear Weapons Free Zone Treaty, pledging not to build, bury, stockpile, or test nuclear weapons.

12

1966 Emmett Ashford becomes the first African American major league umpire.
1968 Black students occupy the administration building at Boston University and demand black history courses and admission of more black students.

13

1907 Harlem Hospital opens in New York City.

14

1775 The first US abolitionist society, the Pennsylvania Society for the Abolition of Slavery, is formed in Philadelphia by Quakers; Benjamin Franklin is its first president.

15

1889 Asa Philip Randolph, labor leader and civil rights advocate, is born in Crescent Way, FL.
1928 Norma Merrick (later Sklarek), first licensed African American female architect in the United States, is born in New York City.

16

1864 Acclaimed singer Flora Batson is born in Washington, DC.
1973 Leila Smith Foley is elected mayor of Taft, OK, becoming the first black woman to serve as mayor of a US city. She will hold the position 13 years.

17

1758 Frances Williams, first African American to graduate from college in the Western Hemisphere, publishes a collection of Latin poems.

18

1818 A regiment of Indians and blacks is defeated in the Battle of Suwanna, FL, ending the first Seminole War.

19

1938 Nana Annor Adjaye, Pan-Africanist, dies in West Nzima, Ghana.

20

1926 Harriet Elizabeth Byrd is born in Cheyenne, WY. A teacher, in 1981 she becomes Wyoming's first black state legislator.
1984 Popular English vocalist Mabel Mercer dies in Pittsfield, MA.

PATRICK HEALY · JESUIT PRIEST, UNIVERSITY PRESIDENT

Patrick Healy is believed to have been the first African American to earn a PhD, and he was the first African American to head a major university. He was one of ten children born to Michael Healy, a transplanted Irishman, and Mary Eliza, a former slave. According to Georgia law, the Healys' children could have been sold as slaves and were prohibited from attending school, but their parents dedicated themselves to providing them with education and opportunity.

Healy (1830–1910) attended a Quaker school in New York and the College of the Holy Cross in Massachusetts. After graduation he joined the Jesuit order, earned his doctorate at the University of Leuven in Belgium, was ordained as a priest, and returned to the United States in 1866 to teach philosophy at Georgetown University in Washington, DC. In 1873 he became the university's twenty-ninth president, a position he held until 1882.

Healy led Georgetown through a period of tremendous growth following the Civil War. He dramatically improved the university's curriculum, emphasizing history and the natural sciences, and began construction of the campus's flagship building. Now a national historic landmark, the magnificent Healy Hall still dominates Georgetown's skyline. Designed in the Flemish Romanesque style—reminiscent of the architecture Healy admired when he studied in Europe—it is a lasting reminder of his outstanding leadership.

Photographer unknown
Prints and Photographs Division, LC-USZ62-48174

INTROSPECTION • PAINTING BY ANITA PHILYAW

Anita Philyaw is a native New Yorker who now lives and paints in Washington, DC. Her vibrant, colorful works, sometimes incorporating collage, are generally set against a background that combines elements of both reality and abstraction. Her paintings depict people of color at work, in motion, or in an introspective moment. In this painting, the young man stops and ponders. He peers out at an unfamiliar world and wonders about his future, a future that for him is uncharted.

Philyaw says, "I paint people in abstract surroundings because, for me, that is the metaphor for the mysteries in life that always surround us. Each of our lives is uniquely individualized, and as individuals we interpret the world as we experience it. We each view and touch life in our own unique style. Still, there is always that place, that common ground, where we recognize one another and join together, communicate with empathy, with love, and with understanding."

Anita Philyaw (American, b. 1937)
Introspection, 2002
Acrylic on canvas, 48.3 x 48.3 cm (19 x 19 in.)
Photograph courtesy Anita Philyaw

APRIL

21
1966 PFC Milton Lee Olive is posthumously awarded the Medal of Honor for bravery during the Vietnam War.

22
1526 The first recorded New World slave revolt occurs in what is now South Carolina.
1922 Bassist, composer, and bandleader Charles Mingus is born in Nogales, AZ.

23
1856 Granville T. Woods, inventor of the steam boiler and automobile air brakes, is born.

24
1993 Oliver Tambo, leader of the African National Congress, dies in Johannesburg.

25
1918 Ella Fitzgerald, "First Lady of Song," is born in Newport News, VA.
1945 The United Nations is founded at a San Francisco meeting attended by W. E. B. Du Bois, Mary McLeod Bethune, Ralph J. Bunche, and Walter White.

26
1991 Maryann Bishop Coffey becomes the first female African American cochair of the National Conference of Christians and Jews.

27
1903 Maggie L. Walker becomes the first black woman to head a bank when she is named president of Richmond's St. Luke Penny Bank and Trust Company.
1994 South Africa's first all-races democratic elections are held.

28
1913 Political activist Margaret Just Butcher is born in Washington, DC.
1957 Chicago lawyer W. Robert Ming is elected chairman of the American Veterans Committee, becoming the first black to head a major national veterans organization.

29
1854 Ashmun Institute (later Lincoln University), the world's first institution founded "to provide a higher education in the arts and sciences for youth of African descent," opens in Oxford, PA.
1992 Four Los Angeles police officers are acquitted of charges stemming from the beating of Rodney King; rioting ensues.

30
1951 Surgeons Rivers Frederick, Ulysses G. Dailey, and Nelson M. Russell are honored by the International College of Surgeons.

APRIL REFLECTIONS

This month I was inspired by:

I'd like to know more about:

The people featured this month and the historical entries brought up these memories:

Next month I would like to:

APRIL REFLECTIONS

RANDOM THOUGHTS

BOOKS TO READ

MUSIC TO HEAR

PERFORMANCES TO SEE

MAY

SUNDAY	MONDAY	TUESDAY	WEDNESDAY	THURSDAY	FRIDAY	SATURDAY
			1	2	3	4	5
○ 6	7	8	9	10	11	◑ 12
13	14	15	16	17	18	19
● 20	21	22	23	24	25	26
27	◐ 28	29	30	31		

MAY   5   CINCO DE MAYO

MAY   7   BANK HOLIDAY (UK)

MAY 13   MOTHER'S DAY

MAY 19   ARMED FORCES DAY

MAY 20   NATIONAL HOLIDAY (UNITED REPUBLIC OF CAMEROON)

MAY 21   VICTORIA DAY (CANADA)

MAY 28   MEMORIAL DAY

HISTORY CLASS, TUSKEGEE INSTITUTE

Founded in 1881, Tuskegee Institute in Tuskegee, Alabama, was established to give newly freed blacks the education and skills needed for economic self-sufficiency. Tuskegee flourished under the leadership of Booker T. Washington, a highly influential leader and educator who espoused the philosophy of "Cast down your bucket where you are." By this he meant progressing through self-help, hard work, and "making friends in every manly way of the people of all races by whom we are surrounded." Washington brought prestige to the school by developing relationships with individuals such as Julius Rosenwald, the man behind Sears, Roebuck & Company, and numerous other wealthy philanthropists, and by recruiting outstanding instructors, including Tuskegee's most notable professor, botanist George Washington Carver. Pictured here are students in a history class, circa 1902.

Today Tuskegee University is one of the nation's top historically black universities. Its campus houses the Tuskegee Institute Historic Site, which includes original buildings constructed by students from bricks made in the school's brickyard. Among Tuskegee's notable alumni are air force pilot General Daniel "Chappie" James, radio host Tom Joyner, singer and instrumentalist Lionel Richie, and Olympic track and field athlete Alice Marie Coachman.

Photograph by Frances Benjamin Johnston
Prints and Photographs Division, LC-USZ62-64712

SEGREGATED DRINKING FOUNTAIN, NORTH CAROLINA

This 1938 photograph of a drinking fountain designated "Colored"—meaning for "colored" people, specifically African Americans—recalls an era when segregation, separate accommodations for African Americans, was the law of the land. It was located on the county courthouse lawn in Halifax, North Carolina. The town of Halifax—the county seat of Halifax County, where laws were established and protected—was in full concurrence with this second-class treatment of its citizens, such as the young boy pictured.

Ironically, Halifax is known as the "Birthplace of Freedom" because the Halifax Resolves, the first official call for independence by a British colony, were adopted there in April 1776. Every year on July 4, residents celebrate their town's initiation of the movement for freedom.

A stone marker has been placed as a memorial on the courthouse lawn where this drinking fountain once stood.

Photograph by John Vachon
Prints and Photographs Division, LC-DIG-fsa-8a03228

MAY

1
1901 Poet, literary critic, and editor Sterling Brown is born in Washington, DC.
1950 Gwendolyn Brooks becomes the first African American to win the Pulitzer Prize, for her book of poetry *Annie Allen*.

2
1969 Record-breaking cricket batsman Brian Lara is born in Santa Cruz, Trinidad.

3
1855 Macon B. Allen becomes the first African American to be formally admitted to the bar in Massachusetts.
1902 Astride Alan-a-Dale, African American jockey Jimmy Winkfield wins his second Kentucky Derby in a row.

4
1942 Songwriter Nickolas Ashford is born in Fairfield, SC. He and his wife, Valerie Simpson, will cowrite many pop hits.
1969 *No Place to Be Somebody* opens in New York. It will win the Pulitzer Prize the following year.

5
1905 Robert Sengstacke Abbott founds *The Chicago Defender*, calling it "the world's greatest weekly."

6
1995 Ron Kirk becomes the first black mayor of Dallas, TX, with 62 percent of the vote.

7
1941 Theodore Browne's play *Natural Man*, a production of the American Negro Theatre, premieres in New York City.
1946 William H. Hastie is inaugurated as the first black governor of the Virgin Islands.

8
1965 The Association for the Advancement of Creative Musicians is founded by Muhal Richard Abrams.

9
1800 John Brown, abolitionist and martyr at Harpers Ferry, is born in Torrington, CT.

10
1968 A public school in Brooklyn, NY, is named for noted scientist and inventor Lewis H. Latimer.

MAY

11 1895 William Grant Still, dean of black classical composers, is born in Woodville, MS.

12 1926 Mervyn Dymally, California's first African American lieutenant governor, is born in Cedros, Trinidad.

13 1914 Heavyweight boxer Joe Louis is born in Lexington, AL.
     1990 George Stallings becomes the Black Catholic Church's first bishop. Stallings broke with the Roman Catholic Church in 1989, citing its failure to meet the needs of black Catholics.

14 1913 Clara Stanton Jones, first black president of the American Library Association, is born in St. Louis, MO.
     1969 John B. McLendon becomes the ABA's first black coach, signing with the Denver Nuggets.
     1999 Washington native Dolores Kendrick is appointed Poet Laureate of the District of Columbia.

15 1918 PFCs Henry Johnson and Needham Roberts become the first Americans to win France's Croix de guerre.
     1946 Camilla Williams appears in the title role of *Madama Butterfly* with the New York City Opera, becoming the first black female singer to sign with a major US opera company.

16 1929 John Conyers Jr., founder of the Congressional Black Caucus, is born in Detroit, MI.

17 1954 The US Supreme Court declares school segregation unconstitutional in *Brown v. Board of Education*.

18 1946 New York Yankees baseball star Reggie Jackson is born in Wyncote, PA. He will set or tie seven World Series records.
     1955 Mary McLeod Bethune, educator and founder of the National Council of Negro Women, dies in Daytona Beach, FL.

19 1993 University of Virginia professor Rita Dove is appointed US Poet Laureate.

20 1868 P. B. S. Pinchback and James J. Harris are named the first African American delegates to the Republican National Convention.

AFRICAN AMERICAN BASEBALL TEAM

In this photograph, taken around 1880, are twenty-three African American men formally dressed in suits, one wearing a top hat and one holding a baseball bat. This baseball team in Danbury, Connecticut, could have been a college team, a minor league team, or a semipro team stocked with ballplayers who would eventually play in the Negro Leagues. Historically, Connecticut was the home of several baseball teams. Many of them were part of the Connecticut State League, a minor league that disbanded after the 1914 season.

The first and most important African American baseball team, the Cuban Giants, once played in the Connecticut State League. The team used the word "Cuban" to disguise the fact that the players were black, and on the field they spoke an unintelligible gibberish meant to sound like Spanish.

Photograph by E. D. Ritton
Prints and Photographs Division, LC-DIG-ppmsca-11502

TOUSSAINT L'OUVERTURE • **HAITIAN PATRIOT, MILITARY LEADER**

Known as the "Liberator of Haiti," Toussaint L'Ouverture (c. 1743–1803) was born François Dominique Toussaint Bréda to slave parents (his father was said to have been an African chief) in Saint-Domingue, a French colony on the Caribbean island of Hispaniola. Toussaint's parents made sure he received a well-rounded education that stressed physical, mental, and spiritual training. In his early thirties Toussaint was given his freedom, married Suzanne Simone Baptiste, and rented a small plantation.

In 1791 discontent with the government's backing of plantation owners led to massive slave revolts in Saint-Domingue. Toussaint joined the army, serving as a doctor and then as a military commander. In 1793 he adopted the name L'Ouverture ("the opener of the way"). Under his leadership, the revolutionaries brought an end to slavery in the French colonies. L'Ouverture became a general, helped defeat invading British troops, and overran Spanish Santo Domingo, abolishing slavery there. On July 1, 1801, L'Ouverture issued a constitution for Saint-Domingue declaring its independence. In 1802 he was betrayed, arrested and sent to France, and imprisoned at Fort-de-Joux, where he died of pneumonia. His lieutenant, Jean-Jacques Dessalines, completed the rebellion, establishing the independent nation of Haiti in 1804.

Le 1er. Juillet 1801, Toussaint L'Ouverture…
Lithograph, artist and date unknown
Prints and Photographs Division, LC-USZ62-7861

MAY

21

1833 African American students enroll in classes at the newly established Oberlin College in Oberlin, OH.

22

1940 Bernard Shaw, journalist and principal Washington anchor for cable news network CNN, is born in Chicago, IL.

1967 Poet Langston Hughes dies in New York City.

23

1832 Jamaican national figure Samuel Sharpe is hanged.

24

1905 Distinguished educator Hilda Davis is born in Washington, DC.

1954 Peter Marshall Murray becomes president of the New York County Medical Society, the first African American physician to head an AMA affiliate.

25

1963 African Liberation Day is declared at the conference of the Organization of African Unity in Addis Ababa, Ethiopia.

2009 Dr. Ivan Van Sertima, Guyana-born scholar, historian, and author of *They Came Before Columbus*, dies in Highland Park, NJ.

26

1926 Renowned jazz trumpeter Miles Davis is born in Alton, IL.

27

1942 Dorie Miller, a messman, is awarded the Navy Cross for heroism at Pearl Harbor.

1958 Ernest Green becomes the first black to graduate from Central High School in Little Rock, AR.

28

1981 Jazz pianist Mary Lou Williams dies in Durham, NC.

29

1973 Tom Bradley becomes the first African American mayor of Los Angeles.

30

1822 Denmark Vesey's conspiracy to free the slaves of Charleston, SC, is thwarted when Peter Prioleau betrays the plot to his master.

1965 Vivian Malone becomes the first black to graduate from the University of Alabama.

31

1931 Mezzo-soprano Shirley Verrett is born in New Orleans. She will become world famous for her performance in *Carmen*.

1955 The US Supreme Court orders school integration "with all deliberate speed."

MAY REFLECTIONS

This month I was inspired by:

I'd like to know more about:

The people featured this month and the historical entries brought up these memories:

Next month I would like to:

MAY REFLECTIONS

RANDOM THOUGHTS

BOOKS TO READ

MUSIC TO HEAR

PERFORMANCES TO SEE

JUNE

SUNDAY	MONDAY	TUESDAY	WEDNESDAY	THURSDAY	FRIDAY	SATURDAY
					1	2
3	○ 4	5	6	7	8	9
10	◑ 11	12	13	14	15	16
17	18	● 19	20	21	22	23
24	25	26	◐ 27	28	29	30

JUN 1   NATIONAL DAY (TUNISIA)

JUN 4   BANK HOLIDAY (UK)

JUN 5   BANK HOLIDAY (UK)
         LIBERATION DAY (SEYCHELLES)

JUN 14 FLAG DAY

JUN 17 FATHER'S DAY

JUN 19 JUNETEENTH

JUN 20 SUMMER SOLSTICE 23:09 UTC
         NATIONAL HOLIDAY (CAMEROON)

JUN 25 NATIONAL DAY (MOZAMBIQUE)

JUN 26 INDEPENDENCE DAY (MADAGASCAR
         AND SOMALIA)

JUN 27 NATIONAL DAY (DJIBOUTI)

JUN 29 INDEPENDENCE DAY (SEYCHELLES)

JUN 30 INDEPENDENCE DAY (ZAIRE)

CONVENTION OF FORMER SLAVES, WASHINGTON, DC

The institution of slavery deprived many generations of blacks of their self-worth, pride, and integrity. But some slaves were not broken by this horrible institution; they were able to keep their dignity, faith, and hope, trusting that they would be freed. Among this group were the participants at the 1916 Annual Convention of Former Slaves. Below is an announcement from the *Washington Post*, September 23, 1916:

> *The fifty-fourth annual convention of "Ex-Slaves" will be held October 22 to October 30, at the Cosmopolitan Baptist Church, this city. The arrangements for the gathering are being made by the White Cross National Colored Old Folks Home Association, which has promised a free dinner to the former slaves, each day of the convention. The Rev. S.P.W. Drew, president and founder of the White Cross organization, is taking an active part in the completion of arrangements. Committees to look after the details of the convention and to make arrangements for housing the delegates were appointed at a mass meeting held last night at Cosmopolitan Church.*

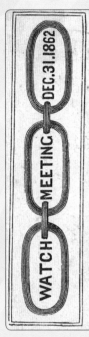

WATCH MEETING, DEC. 31, 1862—WAITING FOR THE HOUR • CARTE DE VISITE PHOTOGRAPH

Juneteenth—June 19—is a day of celebration commemorating the end of slavery in the United States. Although President Lincoln's Emancipation Proclamation became law on January 1, 1863, it was not until June 19, 1865, that Union soldiers arrived in Texas with news that enslaved blacks were now free.

Unlike those who were unaware of their freedom, the slaves depicted in this image are participating in a "watch meeting," watching and waiting for the hour when freedom will be declared. Anticipation was high in these meetings, with prayers and counting of the clock.

When Lincoln freed the slaves, he was concerned that the Emancipation Proclamation might be overturned after the war. To ensure that the evil institution of slavery would never again resurface, Congress proposed and passed the Thirteenth Amendment to the United States Constitution.

Photograph by Heard & Moseley printed on carte de visite mount, c. 1863

Prints and Photographs Division, LC-DIG-ppmsca-10980

JUNE

1   **1919**   Noted physician Caroline Virginia Still Wiley Anderson dies in Philadelphia, PA.

2   **1948**   Jamaican-born track star Herb McKenley sets a new world record for the 400-yard dash.
       1999   Nelson Mandela's successor, Thabo Mbeki, is elected president of South Africa.

3   **1904**   Charles R. Drew, originator of blood plasma banks, is born in Washington, DC.
       2009   Koko Taylor, "Queen of the Blues," dies in Chicago, IL.

4   **1946**   Legislation is enacted authorizing establishment of Mississippi Valley State University in Itta Bena.
       1967   Bill Cosby receives an Emmy Award for his work in the television series *I Spy*.

5   **1973**   Doris A. Davis, mayor of Compton, CA, becomes the first African American woman to govern a city in a major metropolitan area.

6   **1939**   Marian Wright Edelman, the first female African American lawyer in Mississippi and founder of the Children's Defense Fund, is born in Bennettsville, SC.

7   **1917**   Gwendolyn Brooks, US Poet Laureate and teacher, is born in Topeka, KS.
       1994   The Organization of African Unity formally admits South Africa as its 53rd member.

8   **1939**   Herb Adderley, Hall of Famer and defensive back for the Green Bay Packers, is born in Philadelphia, PA.
       1998   Nigerian military ruler Gen. Sani Abacha dies in the nation's capital, Abuja.

9   **1877**   Sculptor Meta Vaux Warrick is born in Philadelphia, PA.
       2000   World-renowned artist Jacob Lawrence dies from lung cancer in Seattle, WA.

10   **1854**   James Augustine Healy, first African American Catholic bishop, is ordained a priest in Notre Dame Cathedral.
       1997   Geronimo Pratt, former Black Panther Party member, is released from jail after serving 27 years for a crime he did not commit.

JUNE

11
1964 Nelson Mandela is sentenced to life imprisonment by the South African government.
2000 Earl T. Shinhoster, prominent civil rights activist who led the NAACP through a difficult period, is killed in a car accident in Alabama.

12
1963 Civil rights activist Medgar Evers is killed in Jackson, MS.

13
1967 Thurgood Marshall is appointed to the US Supreme Court by President Lyndon B. Johnson.
1992 Dominique Dawes makes the US Olympic gymnastics team.

14
1989 Congressman William Gray is elected Democratic whip of the House of Representatives, the highest leadership position in Congress held thus far by an African American.

15
1927 Pianist and composer Natalie Hinderas is born in Oberlin, OH.

16
1976 Students riot in Soweto, South Africa.
1999 In Athens, Greece, Maurice Greene, US track and field athlete, breaks the 100-meter dash world record, running 9.79.

17
1871 James Weldon Johnson, writer, poet, and first African American to be admitted to the Florida bar, is born in Jacksonville, FL.

18
1942 The US Navy commissions its first black officer, Harvard University medical student Bernard Whitfield Robinson.

19
1865 News of the Emancipation Proclamation reaches the South and Texas through Gen. Gordon Granger.

20
1858 Charles Waddell Chesnutt, first African American writer to win literary acclaim in the United States, is born in Cleveland, OH.

SCHOOLCHILDREN VIEWING STATUE OF GEORGE WASHINGTON

President George Washington, the "Father of His Country," is widely memorialized in cities across the United States, including, of course, Washington, DC. Numerous monuments and memorials in his honor are open to the huge number of tourists who visit the nation's capital each year.

This image, captured around 1899 by the pioneering photographer Frances Benjamin Johnston, shows a group of well-dressed African American schoolchildren from Washington, DC, during a visit to the US Capitol. Johnston, whose work paved the way for future female photographers, pursued photography after receiving her first camera from George Eastman of the Eastman Kodak Company; a large collection of her work is housed at the Library of Congress. Around the time of this image, Johnston also created a photographic series documenting the daily life of Hampton Normal and Agricultural Institute in Hampton, Virginia. The series was exhibited at the Exposition Universelle of 1900 in Paris.

The massive thirty-ton statue *Enthroned Washington* was sculpted by Horatio Greenough, who modeled it after the ancient statue *Zeus Olympios*. Commissioned for the centennial of Washington's birth in 1832, it was displayed on the east lawn of the Capitol at the time of this photograph. The statue now resides in the Smithsonian Institution's National Museum of American History.

Photograph by Frances Benjamin Johnston
Prints and Photographs Division, LC-DIG-ppmsc-04904

MATHIAS DE SOUSA • MARINER, FUR TRADER, LEGISLATOR

Mathias de Sousa was the first black citizen of the state of Maryland. His surname indicates that he was of African and Portuguese descent, though he appeared more African in skin color and features. De Sousa arrived as an indentured servant on the ship *The Ark* with Lord Baltimore in 1634. When his indenture was completed four years later, he became a mariner and fur trader. De Sousa was not only a citizen; he served in the legislative assembly of freemen in 1642, making him the first person of African descent to hold political office in the state of Maryland.

The photograph shows part of a memorial plaque at the site of de Sousa's initial landing on Maryland's eastern shore, near the campus of St. Mary's College of Maryland.

Mathias de Sousa marker, Historic St. Mary's City Museum of History and Archaeology, St. Mary's City, Maryland

Photograph courtesy IOKTS Productions

JUNE

21
1859 Renowned painter Henry Ossawa Tanner is born in Pittsburgh, PA.
1998 Marion Jones is the first athlete in 50 years to win the 100- and 200-meter events and long jump at the US Track and Field Championships in Indianapolis, IN.

22
1972 National Black MBA Association is incorporated, with over 2,000 members.

23
1899 Pvt. George Wanton is cited for bravery at Tayabacoa, Cuba, in the Spanish-American War.

24
1877 Bishop Josiah M. Kibira becomes the first black African leader of the Lutheran World Federation.

25
1792 Thomas Peters, an African American slave who led black emigrants from Nova Scotia to settle in Sierra Leone, dies in Freetown.
2009 Michael Jackson, "King of Pop," dies in Los Angeles.

26
1993 Roy Campanella, legendary catcher for the Negro Leagues and the Los Angeles Dodgers, dies in Woodland Hills, CA.

27
1833 Prudence Crandall, a white woman, is arrested for teaching black girls at her academy in Canterbury, CT.
1872 Prominent poet and writer Paul Laurence Dunbar is born in Dayton, OH.

28
1911 Samuel J. Battle becomes the first African American policeman in New York City.

29
1886 Photographer James VanDerZee is born in Lenox, MA.
1998 Atlanta Hawks head coach Lenny Wilkens becomes the second person to be elected to the NBA Hall of Fame twice, as a player and a coach.

30
1917 Actor, singer, and civil rights advocate Lena Horne is born in Brooklyn, NY.

JUNE REFLECTIONS

This month I was inspired by:

I'd like to know more about:

The people featured this month and the historical entries brought up these memories:

Next month I would like to:

JUNE REFLECTIONS

RANDOM THOUGHTS

BOOKS TO READ

MUSIC TO HEAR

PERFORMANCES TO SEE

JULY

SUNDAY	MONDAY	TUESDAY	WEDNESDAY	THURSDAY	FRIDAY	SATURDAY
1	2	○ 3	4	5	6	7
8	9	10	◐ 11	12	13	14
15	16	17	18	● 19	20	21
22	23	24	25	◐ 26	27	28
29	30	31				

JUL	1	CANADA DAY (CANADA) INDEPENDENCE DAY (BURUNDI AND RWANDA)	JUL	10	INDEPENDENCE DAY (BAHAMAS)
JUL	2	CANADA DAY HOLIDAY (CANADA)	JUL	11	PRESIDENT'S DAY (BOTSWANA)
JUL	4	INDEPENDENCE DAY	JUL	12	BANK HOLIDAY (N. IRELAND)
JUL	6	INDEPENDENCE DAY (MALAWI)	JUL	19	RAMADAN (BEGINS AT SUNSET)
JUL	7	SABA SABA DAY (TANZANIA)	JUL	23	ANNIVERSARY OF REVOLUTION (EGYPT)
			JUL	26	INDEPENDENCE DAY (LIBERIA)

CHARLOTTE HOLLOMAN • OPERA SINGER

Charlotte Wesley Holloman was born in 1922 in the Georgetown neighborhood of Washington, DC. Her mother, Florence Louise Johnson Wesley, was a schoolteacher, and her father, Charles Harris Wesley, was a minister and noted historian. Charlotte spent her elementary school years in both Washington, DC, and London, where her father conducted historical research under a Guggenheim Fellowship. In 1937 she graduated from Dunbar High School, one of Washington's premier African American schools.

Her talent in playing the piano was evident at an early age, and at fifteen she entered Howard University to continue her studies. During her senior year she was inspired to study classical voice by Professor Todd Duncan, who played the role of Porgy in George Gershwin's *Porgy and Bess*. With Duncan's mentorship, Holloman developed a masterful singing technique, displayed in her 1954 debut in New York City. She received rave reviews, such as the following from the *Musical Courier:* "To enumerate a few of the attributes observed at this first hearing: she was personable and easy on the stage; she disclosed marked understanding of text and mood color; she possesses a spectacular voice of beautiful timbre which ascended and descended the vocal octaves with exciting ease."

Holloman also performed in musical theater, both on and off Broadway. In 1955 she sang in Harry Belafonte's vocal chorus, and she once sang background vocals for James Brown. She is pictured here in 1957.

Photograph by Carl Van Vechten
Prints and Photographs Division, LC-USZ62-114441

THE UNEMPLOYED, CHARLESTON • ETCHING BY ELIZABETH O'NEILL VERNER

The men depicted in this etching evoke similar scenes of the present day. Work was hard to find during the Great Depression of the 1930s, just as the economic downturn of the late 2000s caused unemployment levels to increase significantly. Similarly, black unemployed workers of the 1930s had it harder than most and had to take whatever work would come their way.

Charleston, South Carolina, had been one of several southern cities in which the African American community prospered, establishing businesses, law offices, pharmacies, and so forth, and even had congressional representation. The most noted congressman of the time was Joseph Hayne Rainey (1832–1887), the first black to serve in the US House of Representatives. When the Reconstruction period ended, however, in the late nineteenth century, blacks had to begin anew in establishing equality in this country.

Elizabeth O'Neill Verner (American, 1883–1979)
The Unemployed, Charleston, c. 1930
Etching
Prints and Photographs Division, LC-USZ62-83755

JULY

1
1899 Rev. Thomas Dorsey, "Father of Gospel Music," is born in Villa Rica, GA.
1975 Wallace D. Muhammad, head of the Nation of Islam, opens the group to members of all races.

2
1908 Thurgood Marshall, first African American US Supreme Court justice, is born in Baltimore, MD.
1999 Alexandra Stevenson, daughter of NBA star Julius Erving, is the first qualifier to advance to the semifinals of the Wimbledon tennis tournament in England.

3
1962 Jackie Robinson becomes the first African American to be inducted into the National Baseball Hall of Fame.

4
1881 Tuskegee Institute opens in Tuskegee, AL, with Booker T. Washington as its first president.

5
1809 Eighteen blacks under the leadership of Reverend Thomas Paul establish the Abyssinian Baptist Church in New York City.
1892 Andrew Beard is issued a patent for the rotary engine.

6
1993 Eleven lives are lost in an antigovernment riot in Lagos, Nigeria.

7
1993 Political violence in South Africa continues after the declaration of the nation's first all-races democratic election.

8
1943 Women's rights advocate Faye Wattleton is born in St. Louis, MO.
2000 Venus Williams defeats Lindsay Davenport 6–3, 7–6, to win her first Wimbledon tennis championship.

9
1936 Poet and author June Jordan is born in Harlem, NY.

10
1993 Kenyan runner Yobes Ondieki is the first man to run 10,000 meters in under 27 minutes.

JULY

11   **1915**   Mifflin Wistar Gibbs, first African American to be elected a municipal judge, dies in Little Rock, AR.

12   **1937**   William Cosby, EdD, comedian, actor, educator, and humanitarian, is born in Philadelphia, PA.

13   **1928**   Robert N. C. Nix Jr., first African American chief justice of a state supreme court (Pennsylvania), is born in Philadelphia, PA.

14   **1996**   In Lapeenranta, Finland, Kenyan runner Daniel Komen shaves almost four seconds off the world mile record.

15   **1929**   Francis Bebey, guitarist and author, is born in Douala, Cameroon.

16   **1882**   Violette Anderson, first African American woman to practice before the US Supreme Court, is born in London.
       1998   Dr. John Henrik Clarke, historian and scholar, dies in New York City.

17   **1911**   Frank Snowden Jr., foremost scholar on blacks in antiquity, is born in York County, VA.

18   **1896**   First African American professional golfer, John Shippen, finishes fifth in the US Open.
       1899   L. C. Bailey is issued a patent for the folding bed.

19   **1979**   In her second Cabinet-level appointment, Patricia Roberts Harris is named secretary of health and human services.

20   **1967**   The first National Conference of Black Power opens in Newark, NJ.

WILLIAM LACY CLAY SR. • US CONGRESSMAN

William Lacy Clay (American, b. 1931), a native of St. Louis, Missouri, was first elected to the US House of Representatives in 1968. At the time of his retirement in 2001, he was the senior member of the Missouri congressional delegation and ranked third in seniority in the House. He served as the ranking Democrat on the Committee on Education and Labor, where he played an instrumental role in authorizing the 1998 Amendments to the Higher Education Act, the Carl D. Perkins Vocational and Technical Education Act of 1998, and other significant legislation furthering education.

Clay founded a nonprofit, tax-exempt scholarship and research funding program that has enabled more than a hundred students from the St. Louis area to attend colleges nationwide. He earned his bachelor of science degree in history and political science from St. Louis University and is the recipient of eleven honorary degrees for his thirty-two years as a legislator.

Photograph courtesy Vicki Clay

SEGREGATED MOVIE THEATER, MISSISSIPPI

In the segregated South and some parts of the North, blacks were not permitted to use the front entrance of theaters. Typically restricted to balcony seating, they were forced to enter the theater through a back or side entrance, as seen in this photograph taken in 1939 in Belzoni, Mississippi Delta, Mississippi. The situation prompted African American businessmen to open theaters for blacks within their own communities to spare them this humiliation.

Some of the better-known theaters operated by African Americans were the Regal Theater in Chicago; the Grand Theater in Charlotte, North Carolina; the Apollo Theater in New York City; and the Lincoln Theatre in Washington, DC.

Photograph by Marion Post Wolcott
Prints and Photographs Division, LC-DIG-ppmsca-12888

JULY

21   **1896**   Mary Church Terrell founds the National Association of Colored Women in Washington, DC.

22   **1939**   Jane Bolin is appointed to New York City's Domestic Relations Court, becoming the first female African American judge.

23   **1900**   The first Pan-African Congress, organized by Henry Sylvester Williams, is held in London.

24   **1925**   Operatic soprano Adele Addison is born in New York City.

25   **1916**   Wearing the protective mask he invented, Garrett Morgan enters a gas-filled tunnel with a rescue party after an underground explosion in Cleveland, OH; six lives are saved.

26   **1865**   Catholic priest Patrick Francis Healy becomes the first African American to earn a PhD degree.

27   **1996**   Donovan Bailey, a Jamaican running for Canada, becomes the "world's fastest human" in the Atlanta Olympics, setting a world record of 9.84 in the 100-meter dash.

28   **1868**   The 14th Amendment is ratified, granting citizenship to African Americans.
       1996   Ethiopian police officer Fatuma Roba becomes the first African woman to win a medal in an Olympic marathon.

29   **1909**   Crime novelist Chester Himes is born in Jefferson City, MO.

30   **1996**   Three years after recovering from third-degree burns, Cuba's Ana Quirot wins a silver medal in the 800-meter run in the Atlanta Olympics.

31   **1921**   Educator and civil rights activist Whitney Young Jr. is born in Lincoln Ridge, KY.

JULY REFLECTIONS

This month I was inspired by:

I'd like to know more about:

The people featured this month and the historical entries brought up these memories:

Next month I would like to:

JULY REFLECTIONS

RANDOM THOUGHTS

BOOKS TO READ

MUSIC TO HEAR

PERFORMANCES TO SEE

AUGUST

SUNDAY	MONDAY	TUESDAY	WEDNESDAY	THURSDAY	FRIDAY	SATURDAY
			1	○ 2	3	4
5	6	7	8	◐ 9	10	11
12	13	14	15	16	● 17	18
19	20	21	22	23	◐ 24	25
26	27	28	29	30	○ 31	

AUG 1   EMANCIPATION DAY (JAMAICA)

AUG 3   INDEPENDENCE DAY (NIGER)

AUG 6   CIVIC HOLIDAY (CANADA, MOST PROVINCES)
BANK HOLIDAY (SCOTLAND)
INDEPENDENCE DAY (JAMAICA)

AUG 11   INDEPENDENCE DAY (CHAD)

AUG 13   INDEPENDENCE DAY
(CENTRAL AFRICAN REPUBLIC)

AUG 15   NATIONAL DAY (REPUBLIC OF THE CONGO)

AUG 16   RESTORATION DAY (DOMINICAN REPUBLIC)

AUG 17   INDEPENDENCE DAY (GABON)

AUG 18   EID-AL-FITR (BEGINS AT SUNSET)

AUG 24   NATIONAL FLAG DAY (LIBERIA)

AUG 27   BANK HOLIDAY (UK EXCEPT SCOTLAND)

AUG 30   FÊTE LA ROSE (FEAST OF ST. ROSE OF LIMA),
ST. LUCIA

AUG 31   INDEPENDENCE DAY (TRINIDAD AND TOBAGO)

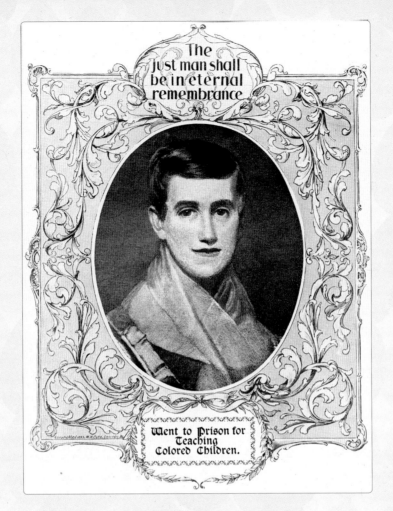

The
just man shall
be in eternal
remembrance

Went to Prison for
Teaching
Colored Children.

Copyrighted 1893, W.H.Cole, Chicago, Ill.

PRUDENCE CRANDALL • EDUCATOR

Prudence Crandall (1803–1890) was born in Hopkinton, Rhode Island, to Quaker parents; the family later moved to Canterbury, Connecticut. In 1831 Prudence purchased a female boarding academy in Canterbury with her sister, Almira. The school, catering to daughters of wealthy local families, was highly successful in its first year.

The following fall Crandall admitted a young African American woman to the academy. Sarah Harris, the daughter of a free African American farmer, wanted an education that would prepare her to teach other African Americans. In response to Harris's admittance, white parents withdrew their daughters. Crandall temporarily closed the school and recruited African American students from free black communities throughout New England; in April 1833 she reopened the academy for the "reception of young Ladies and little Misses of color." Community outrage followed, and Connecticut passed the "Black Law," making it illegal to educate out-of-state African Americans without the town's permission. Crandall was arrested, jailed overnight, and released on bond to await trial. She continued operating the academy throughout the judicial process despite increasing hostility and violence. On the third trial the case was dismissed; two months later a mob set fire to the school. For her students' safety, Crandall ceased operations.

In 1838 Connecticut repealed the Black Law, and in 1995 Crandall was declared official state heroine for her courage and moral strength in taking a stand against prejudice. Today the Prudence Crandall Museum in Canterbury, operated by the Connecticut Historical Commission, is a national historic landmark.

AFRICAN AMERICAN CHILDREN PLAYING GOLF

This photograph from the Detroit Publishing Company, taken around 1905, was a gift to the Library of Congress from the State Historical Society of Colorado. It depicts black children preparing to hit a golf ball on a tee. The location is unknown, as is the origin of the idea that young black children at the turn of the twentieth century would be hitting golf balls as a play activity.

African Americans have had a distinguished presence in golf, however, dating back to 1896, when John Shippen Jr. played in the second US Open. Shippen, who became a professional and played in five other US Opens, learned the game from a Scottish player who had come to Long Island, New York, to build a golf course on the Shinnecock Indian Reservation. Dr. George Franklin Grant, a dentist and professor at Harvard University, invented the wooden golf tee and patented it in 1899. Many other African Americans have made golfing history, among them Charlie Sifford, the first African American PGA Tour member; Bill Powell, the first African American to design, build, and operate his own golf course; Lee Elder, the first African American to play in the Masters Tournament; and Renee Powell (daughter of Bill Powell), the second woman to qualify for the LPGA Tour and recipient of the Professional Golfers' Association's First Lady of Golf Award.

Photographer unknown
Prints and Photographs Division, LC-DIG-det-4a12570

AUGUST

1   **1996**   At the Summer Olympics in Atlanta, Michael Johnson becomes the first man to win gold medals in both the 200- and 400-meter runs, breaking his own world record in the 200.

2   **1847**   William A. Leidesdorff launches the first steamboat in San Francisco Bay.
      1997   Nigerian musician and political activist Fela Anikulapo-Kuti dies from AIDS in Lagos.

3   **1996**   Josia Thugwane becomes the first black South African to win an Olympic gold medal, completing the marathon in 2 hours, 12 minutes, 36 seconds.

4   **1961**   Barack Obama, future president of the United States, is born in Honolulu, HI.
      1997   Australia's Cathy Freeman becomes the first aboriginal athlete to capture a world track title when she wins the 400-meter event in Greece.

5   **1914**   The first electric traffic lights (invented by Garrett Morgan) are installed in Cleveland, OH.

6   **1965**   President Lyndon B. Johnson signs the Voting Rights Act, outlawing the literacy test for voting eligibility in the South.

7   **1904**   Ralph Bunche, first African American Nobel Prize winner, is born in Detroit, MI.

8   **1865**   Matthew A. Henson, first explorer to reach the North Pole, is born in Charles County, MD.

9   **1936**   Jesse Owens wins four gold medals in track and field events at the Berlin Olympics.
      2003   Gregory Hines, actor and dancer, dies from cancer in Los Angeles.

10   **1829**   A race riot erupts in Cincinnati, OH, prompting about 1,000 blacks to leave for Canada, Michigan, western Pennsylvania, and New York.
      1989   Gen. Colin Powell is nominated as chairman of the Joint Chiefs of Staff.
      2008   Isaac Hayes, singer, songwriter, and actor, dies in Memphis, TN.

AUGUST

11   **1921**   Alex Haley, author, is born in Ithaca, NY.

12   **1890**   Acclaimed soprano Lillian Evans Evanti, first African American to perform with an organized European opera company, is born in Washington, DC. In 1934 she gives a command performance for President Franklin Roosevelt at the White House.

13   **1989**   The wreckage of the plane that carried US congressman Mickey Leland and others on a humanitarian mission is found on a mountainside in Ethiopia; there are no survivors.
       2007   Educator and historian Asa Hilliard III dies in Cairo, Egypt.

14   **1990**   Singer Curtis Mayfield is paralyzed in an accident at an outdoor concert in Brooklyn, NY.

15   **1938**   Maxine Waters, second African American woman from California to be elected to Congress, is born in St. Louis, MO.

16   **1930**   Innovative blues guitarist Robert Johnson dies in Greenwood, MS.
       1998   Harlem Renaissance author Dorothy West dies in Boston, MA.

17   **1993**   Jackie Joyner-Kersee wins her 17th consecutive heptathlon at the World Track and Field Championships in Stuttgart, Germany.

18   **1963**   James Meredith becomes the first African American to graduate from the University of Mississippi.

19   **1989**   Bishop Desmond Tutu defies apartheid laws by walking alone on a South Africa beach.

20   **1565**   Black artisans and farmers aid the explorer Pedro Menéndez de Avilés in building St. Augustine, FL.
       1619   The first group of 20 Africans is brought to Jamestown, VA.

SEA TO SHINING SEA • SILKSCREEN BY LOU STOVALL

In 2008 the master printmaker Lou Stovall (American, b. 1937) was one of many inspired artists who created a vision marking the impending historic moment when the first African American would be elected president of the United States.

Stovall explains: "Hearing Senator Barack Obama emphatically state, 'I want to end the mindset that got us into war in the first place,' I was moved to hope that the next President of the United States would share my belief in the possibility of world peace. I immediately began to make a work of art to support Senator Obama's ideals and, more practically, his campaign." In making *Sea to Shining Sea,* Stovall "employed elements of America's landscape—the same elements referenced by artists, poets, writers and musicians to inspire patriotism and positive ambition in our children . . . The purple mountains, verdant green hills and rich, deep brown soil support 'amber waves of grain' . . . Above the tree limbs, vibrantly colored birds soar with wings intertwined. Though each is very different, the birds share their flight peacefully and lovingly . . . It is my dream that Senator Obama will unite our diverse nation so that we may enjoy our freedoms while respecting one another. My hope floats quietly yet passionately on ripples and waves 'from sea to shining sea.' I believe Senator Obama will bring a tide of change, altering the fundamental direction of our world."

Lou Stovall (American, b. 1937)
Sea to Shining Sea, 2008
Silkscreen, 50.7 x 50.7 cm (20 x 20 in.)
Prints and Photographs Division, LC-DIG-ds-00043

POWHATAN BEATY • SOLDIER, ACTOR

Powhatan Beaty (American, 1837–1916) was first and foremost a courageous Union soldier during the Civil War. He fought in more than thirteen battles and led an elite all-black fighting brigade. But privately Beaty trained to become a successful actor and powerful orator.

Beaty was born into slavery in Richmond, Virginia, gained his freedom, and was educated in Cincinnati, Ohio, where he developed an interest in theater. At the age of twenty-four he enlisted in the Union Army. Serving in the Fifth United States Colored Infantry, Beaty distinguished himself with his bravery, skill, and leadership in battle after battle. On September 29, 1864, at the Battle of Chaffin's Farm in Virginia, First Sergeant Beaty led a depleted company to victory, uprooting a well-entrenched battalion of Confederate troops. For his conduct during this battle Beaty was awarded the Congressional Medal of Honor.

After his military service Beaty resumed his acting career, appearing in various small roles and engaging in public speaking in the Cincinnati black community. His most impressive dramatic work was with the renowned African American actress Henrietta Vinton Davis. The critical acclaim that Beaty and Davis received for their portrayal of Macbeth and Lady Macbeth brought them an opportunity to perform Shakespeare again at Ford's Opera House in Washington, DC. Beaty and Davis performed brilliantly to a full house; the audience of more than 1,100 people included Frederick Douglass.

AUGUST

21
1904 Bandleader and composer William "Count" Basie is born in Red Bank, NJ.

22
1910 The famous Howard Theater in Washington, DC, opens for Broadway shows and musical entertainment.
1978 Kenyan president and revolutionary Jomo Kenyatta dies in Mombasa.

23
1900 Booker T. Washington forms the National Negro Business League in Boston, MA.

24
1903 Pianist and bandleader Claude Hopkins is born in Alexandria, VA.

25
1989 Huey P. Newton, cofounder of the Black Panther Party, dies in Oakland, CA.

26
1946 Composer, singer, and producer Valerie Simpson is born in the Bronx, NY.

27
1937 Alice Coltrane, musician, is born in Detroit, MI.
1963 W. E. B. Du Bois, scholar, civil rights activist, and founding father of the NAACP, dies in Accra, Ghana.

28
1963 A quarter million demonstrators take part in the March on Washington for Jobs and Freedom, the largest civil rights demonstration to date in US history.

29
1920 Jazz saxophonist Charlie "Bird" Parker is born in Kansas City, KS.

30
1800 Gabriel Prosser, a slave, organizes a slave revolt in Virginia.
1983 Lt. Col. Guion S. Bluford Jr. becomes the first African American in space.

31
1935 Baseball player and manager Frank Robinson is born in Beaufort, TX.

AUGUST REFLECTIONS

This month I was inspired by:

I'd like to know more about:

The people featured this month and the historical entries brought up these memories:

Next month I would like to:

AUGUST REFLECTIONS

RANDOM THOUGHTS

BOOKS TO READ

MUSIC TO HEAR

PERFORMANCES TO SEE

SEPTEMBER

SUNDAY	MONDAY	TUESDAY	WEDNESDAY	THURSDAY	FRIDAY	SATURDAY
						1
2	3	4	5	6	7	◑ 8
9	10	11	12	13	14	15
● 16	17	18	19	20	21	◐ 22
23	24	25	26	27	28	29
○ 30						

SEP   1   HEROES DAY (TANZANIA)

SEP   3   LABOR DAY (US, CANADA)

SEP   6   INDEPENDENCE DAY (SWAZILAND)

SEP   7   INDEPENDENCE DAY (BRAZIL)

SEP   10   NATIONAL DAY (BELIZE)

SEP   12   INDEPENDENCE DAY (CAPE VERDE)

SEP   16   ROSH HASHANAH (BEGINS AT SUNSET)
INDEPENDENCE DAY (PAPUA NEW GUINEA)

SEP   17   NATIONAL HEROES DAY (ANGOLA)

SEP   21   INTERNATIONAL DAY OF PEACE
INDEPENDENCE DAY (BELIZE)

SEP   22   AUTUMNAL EQUINOX 14:49 UTC
INDEPENDENCE DAY (MALI)

SEP   24   REPUBLIC DAY (TRINIDAD)

SEP   25   YOM KIPPUR (BEGINS AT SUNSET)
REFERENDUM DAY (RWANDA)

SEP   30   INDEPENDENCE DAY (BOTSWANA)

"WELL, NATURALLY I BELIEVE IN NONVIOLENCE, BUT THE COPS DON'T SEEM TO KNOW THAT!" • CARTOON BY OLIVER HARRINGTON

Oliver Wendell Harrington (1912–1995) was the first syndicated black cartoonist to achieve national recognition. He was born in Valhalla, New York, graduated from the Yale School of Fine Arts, and worked for several leading black newspapers, including the *Pittsburgh Courier* and the *Chicago Defender*. His cartoon series *Dark Laughter,* which debuted in the *Amsterdam News* in 1935, featured his most famous character, Bootsie. Through Bootsie, Harrington critiqued various social issues of his time, such as the Vietnam War, Watergate, and the treatment of African Americans in the United States. This *Dark Laughter* cartoon shows Bootsie, head wrapped in bandages, standing at a bar talking about an injury he received from police at a civil rights demonstration.

Feeling the heat from the House Un-American Activities Committee, in 1951 Harrington fled to Europe, where he met other notable American expatriates, including writers Chester Himes and Richard Wright. In 1961 Harrington moved to East Berlin, where he found work illustrating magazines and cartooning. He spent the rest of his life there, unable to cross the Berlin Wall. Poet Langston Hughes called Harrington "the greatest African American cartoonist."

Oliver Wendell Harrington (American, 1912–1995)
Dark Laughter cartoon published in the *Pittsburgh Courier,* December 19, 1964
Crayon, ink, and pencil drawing
Prints and Photographs Division, LC-DIG-ppmsca-10840

McDOUGALD'S DRUG STORE, ATLANTA, GEORGIA

Atlanta, Georgia, has long been a mecca for African American economic progress. It is a city where African Americans have prospered since the Emancipation Proclamation freed the slaves.

The citizens of Atlanta have been a key part of the nation's history, with Sherman's March to the Sea during the Civil War, the Atlanta race riot of 1906, and the Great Atlanta Fire of 1917. The fire destroyed entire blocks, including much of the Sweet Auburn district, where black progress was ubiquitous. This was the neighborhood of Dr. Martin Luther King Jr. and his family.

Many African Americans in major cities across America have been business owners, such as Atlanta's Dr. J. F. McDougald, proprietor of the drugstore pictured here around 1900; they have also practiced law, medicine, dentistry, and banking. Curiously, also as in Atlanta, African American prosperity has often ignited race riots that destroyed entire communities. This has been evident in cities such as Chicago, Illinois; Wilmington, North Carolina; and Tulsa, Oklahoma.

Photographer unknown
Prints and Photographs Division, LC-USZ62-69

SEPTEMBER

1

1993 Condoleezza Rice is named provost at Stanford University, becoming the youngest person and the first black to hold this position.

2

1833 Ohio's Oberlin College, first US college to routinely enroll black students, is founded.
1975 Joseph W. Hatcher becomes Florida's first African American supreme court justice since Reconstruction.

3

1838 Frederick Douglass escapes from slavery, disguised as a sailor.

4

1957 Arkansas governor Orval Faubus calls out the National Guard to bar African American students from entering a high school in Little Rock.

5

1960 Léopold Sédar Senghor, poet and politician, is elected president of Senegal.

6

1996 Eddie Murray joins Hank Aaron and Willie Mays as the only baseball players with at least 500 home runs and 3,000 hits.

7

1927 Dolores Kendrick, future Poet Laureate of the District of Columbia, is born in Washington, DC.
1954 Integration of public schools begins in Washington, DC, and Baltimore, MD.

8

1766 Joseph Boulogne Saint-George participates in his first public fencing match in Paris.
1981 Roy Wilkins, executive director of the NAACP, dies in New York City.

9

1915 Dr. Carter G. Woodson founds the Association for the Study of Negro Life and History.
1999 A Texas jury imposes the death sentence on Lawrence Russell Brewer, the second white supremacist convicted of killing James Byrd Jr.

10

1961 Jomo Kenyatta returns to Kenya from exile, during which he had been elected president of the Kenya National African Union.

SEPTEMBER

11
1974   Haile Selassie I is deposed from the Ethiopian throne.
1999   Seventeen-year-old Serena Williams defeats Martina Hingis to win her first major tennis championship, the US Open.

12
1913   Track and field star Jesse Owens is born in Oakville, AL.
1977   Stephen Biko, leader of the black consciousness movement in South Africa, dies in police custody in Pretoria.

13
1913   Dancer, Tony Award winner, and famed Motown choreographer Cholly Atkins is born in Pratt City, AL.

14
1980   Dorothy Boulding Ferebee, physician and second president of the National Council for Negro Women, dies in Washington, DC.

15
1830   The first national convention for blacks is held at Bethel Church, Philadelphia, PA.
1943   Paul Robeson performs in *Othello* for the 269th time.

16
1925   Blues great B. B. King is born in Indianola, MS.

17
1983   Vanessa Williams, Miss New York, becomes the first black Miss America.

18
1980   Cosmonaut Arnoldo Tamayo, a Cuban, becomes the first black to travel in space.

19
1963   Iota Phi Theta fraternity is founded at Morgan State University, Baltimore, MD.
1989   Gordon Parks's *Learning Tree* is among the first films listed on the National Film Registry of the Library of Congress.

20
1664   Maryland takes the lead in passing laws against the marriage of English women to black men.
1830   The National Negro Convention convenes in Philadelphia, PA, with the purpose of abolishing slavery.

GEORGE WASHINGTON CARVER • SCIENTIST, BOTANIST, INVENTOR, EDUCATOR

George Washington Carver (American, c. 1864–1943) was world renowned for his achievements in agricultural research. In 1896, having completed his master's degree in botany, Carver was invited by Booker T. Washington, founder of the Tuskegee Normal and Industrial Institute (later Tuskegee University), to head the institute's agriculture department. Carver held the position for nearly five decades. He taught southern sharecroppers and farmers how to grow and preserve nutritious foods and how to maximize their yield by rotating crops. In 1914, when the boll weevil threatened cotton production in the South, Carver suggested that farmers look to other crops as sources of income. He demonstrated the value of plants that were not currently grown, such as peanuts and sweet potatoes, by developing processes for manufacturing paper, ink, shaving cream, linoleum, synthetic rubber, plastics, bleach, metal polish, and more than three hundred other consumer and industrial products from them. His advice was sought by people around the globe, including Mahatma Gandhi, Joseph Stalin, and automobile magnate Henry Ford. Carver's development of peanut milk as a more nutritious alternative to cow's milk saved the lives of hundreds of babies in West Africa.

Carver once expressed his spiritual connection with plants: "How do I talk to a little flower? Through it I talk to the Infinite . . . When you look into the heart of a rose, there you experience it."

Photograph by Frances Benjamin Johnston

Courtesy IOKTS Productions

BLACK PILOTS OF THE ARMY AIR FORCES

On March 7, 1942, the first five black cadets were commissioned as pilots in the United States Army Air Forces. All had been students of the Tuskegee Flight Training Program, which operated at Tuskegee Institute under the Civilian Pilot Training Program. In the program, blacks had the opportunity to study aviation under the tutelage of such great flyers as Cornelius Coffey, C. Alfred "Chief" Anderson, Frederick Patterson, and George L. Washington.

Women were included as students of the rigorous program, perhaps inspired by the legacy of Bessie Coleman, the first African American to earn an international pilot's license. This photograph includes some of the most notable female graduates of Tuskegee's flight program. Left to right, they are Lola Jones, Willa Brown (standing in back), Doris Murphy, and Janet Harmon Waterford Bragg; the aviator at far right is unidentified. Janet Bragg, who was also a registered nurse, and Willa Brown were among the founding members of the National Airmen's Association of America.

Photograph courtesy National Archives

SEPTEMBER

21
1998 Florence "Flo-Jo" Griffith-Joyner, Olympic gold medalist in track, dies at 39 from an apparent heart seizure in Mission Viejo, CA.
2008 President Thabo Mbeki of South Africa resigns from office.

22
1828 Zulu leader Shaka the Great is assassinated.
1915 Xavier University, the first African American Catholic college, opens in New Orleans.

23
1993 South Africa's parliament creates a multiracial body to oversee the end of exclusive white control of the nation.

24
1923 Nancy Green, the world's first living trademark (Aunt Jemima), is struck and killed by an automobile in Chicago, IL.

25
1911 Dr. Eric Williams, future prime minister of Trinidad and Tobago, is born in Port of Spain.
1974 Barbara W. Hancock becomes the first African American woman to be named a White House Fellow.

26
1937 Bessie Smith, "Empress of the Blues," dies in Clarksdale, MS.
1998 Betty Carter, jazz singer, dies from pancreatic cancer in New York City.

27
1944 Stephanie Pogue, artist and professor, is born in Shelby, NC.

28
1829 David Walker, a freeborn black, publishes a provocative pamphlet calling for slaves worldwide to revolt against their white masters.
1912 W. C. Handy's "Memphis Blues" is published.

29
1980 The Schomburg Center for Research in Black Culture opens a new $3.8 million building in New York City.
1997 Brazil mercifully agrees to accept thousands of African refugees fleeing war in Angola.

30
1935 Singer Johnny Mathis is born in Gilmer, TX.

SEPTEMBER REFLECTIONS

This month I was inspired by:

I'd like to know more about:

The people featured this month and the historical entries brought up these memories:

Next month I would like to:

SEPTEMBER REFLECTIONS

RANDOM THOUGHTS

BOOKS TO READ

MUSIC TO HEAR

PERFORMANCES TO SEE

OCTOBER

SUNDAY	MONDAY	TUESDAY	WEDNESDAY	THURSDAY	FRIDAY	SATURDAY
		1	2	3	4	5	6
7	◑ 8	9	10	11	12	13
14	● 15	16	17	18	19	20
21	◐ 22	23	24	25	26	27
28	○ 29	30	31			

OCT 1   INDEPENDENCE DAY (NIGERIA)

OCT 4   INDEPENDENCE DAY (LESOTHO)

OCT 8   COLUMBUS DAY
THANKSGIVING DAY (CANADA)

OCT 9   INDEPENDENCE DAY (UGANDA)

OCT 14   YOUNG PEOPLE'S DAY (DEMOCRATIC REPUBLIC OF THE CONGO)

OCT 17   MOTHER'S DAY (MALAWI)

OCT 24   UNITED NATIONS DAY

OCT 25   EID-AL-ADHA (BEGINS AT SUNSET)
INDEPENDENCE DAY (ZAMBIA)

OCT 28   SUMMER TIME ENDS (UK)

OCT 31   HALLOWEEN

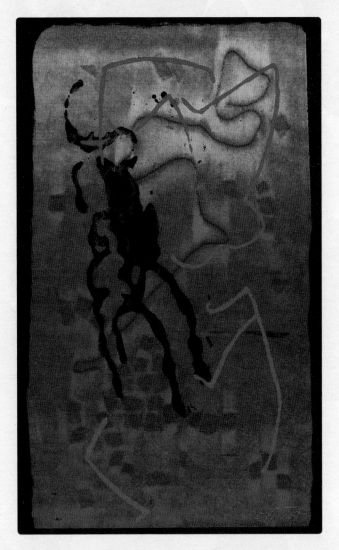

VOODOO DANCE • **SERIGRAPH BY LEONARD PYTLAK**

This serigraph by American artist Leonard Pytlak references a common ritual in the practice of voodoo. Originating in Haiti, voodoo may have roots in West African religious practices. It is often called "black magic," given its elements of the casting of spells, use of voodoo dolls, and belief in the existence of zombies.

Pytlak (1910–1998) was a printmaker who studied at the Newark School of Fine and Industrial Art and at the Art Students League of New York. His silkscreens and lithographs (the medium in which he principally worked) can be viewed in museums and libraries in the United States and England. During the Great Depression years, Pytlak's work was published by the WPA (Works Progress Administration) in New York. The WPA was part of Franklin D. Roosevelt's New Deal, which aided many African American artists and society at large with projects designed to stimulate the American economy.

Leonard Pytlak (American, 1910–1998)

Voodoo Dance, c. 1950–1955

Serigraph on paper, 47 x 31 cm (18½ x 12½ in.)

Prints and Photographs Division, LC-DIG-ppmsca-22079

MAHALIA JACKSON · SINGER

Mahalia Jackson (American, 1911–1972), the "Queen of Gospel Music," was born in New Orleans, where music was an important and ever-present part of the community. Raised by her aunt after her mother died when she was only four, she wasn't allowed to listen to secular music. So with her strong, melodic voice she sang the gospel hymns that her aunt favored, quickly gaining a captive audience in her family and members of the local church choir.

As Jackson searched for her own style, she was influenced by blues singers such as Bessie Smith, Ma Rainey, and Ida Cox, developing a soulful, bluesy sound that was not accepted in some churches. Nevertheless, she continued on. Her beautiful contralto voice was perfected, and her popularity began to soar when she sang with the "Father of Gospel Music," Thomas A. Dorsey. It was Dorsey who wrote her signature song, "Take My Hand, Precious Lord."

Jackson sang to packed houses around the world, at jazz festivals, and on television, and in 1961 she sang for President John F. Kennedy's inaugural ball. She was a major inspiration to Dr. Martin Luther King Jr. during the civil rights protests. In 1968, at the funeral of Dr. King his family requested that Jackson sing his favorite song, "Take My Hand, Precious Lord."

Mahalia Jackson's voice is still revered today and is arguably the most recognizable gospel voice ever heard. Jackson is pictured here at the 1957 Prayer Pilgrimage for Freedom in Washington, DC.

Photographer unknown
Prints and Photographs Division, LC-USZ62-119977

OCTOBER

1

1903 Virginia Proctor Powell, the first professionally trained female African American librarian, is born in Wilkinsburg, PA.

1996 Lt. Gen. Joe Ballard becomes the first African American to head the US Army Corps of Engineers.

2

1958 The Republic of Guinea, under Ahmed Sékou Touré, gains independence from France.

3

1990 Rio de Janeiro's first black congresswoman, Benedita da Silva, sweeps the first round of the city's mayoral race.

4

1943 H. Rap Brown, chairman of the Student Nonviolent Coordinating Committee (SNCC), is born in Baton Rouge, LA.

5

1878 George B. Vashon, first African American lawyer in the state of New York, dies in Rodney, MS.

6

1917 Fannie Lou Hamer, founder of the Mississippi Freedom Democratic Party, is born in Montgomery County, MS.

7

1993 Author Toni Morrison becomes the first African American to win the Nobel Prize in Literature.

8

1820 Henri Christophe, leader of Haitian independence from France, dies in Cap-Haïtien.

1941 Rev. Jesse L. Jackson, political activist and civil rights leader, is born in Greenville, SC.

1980 Bob Marley collapses during a concert in Pittsburgh, PA; he will not perform again.

9

1806 Mathematician and astronomer Benjamin Banneker dies in Ellicott City, MD.

10

1901 Frederick Douglass Patterson, founder of the United Negro College Fund, is born in Washington, DC.

1935 George Gershwin's *Porgy and Bess* premieres at Alvin Theater, New York City.

OCTOBER

11
1792 Antoine Blanc founds the first black Catholic order of nuns.
1919 Jazz drummer and bandleader Art Blakey is born in Pittsburgh, PA.

12
1932 Comedian and civil rights activist Dick Gregory is born in St. Louis, MO.

13
1902 Arna Bontemps, poet and librarian, is born in Alexandria, LA.
1925 Garland Anderson's *Appearances*, the first full-length Broadway play by an African American, opens at the Frolic Theater.

14
1964 Dr. Martin Luther King Jr. is awarded the Nobel Peace Prize.

15
1968 Wyomia Tyus becomes the first person to win the gold medal in the 100-meter race in two consecutive Olympic games.

16
1995 The Million Man March, "A Day of Atonement," takes place in Washington, DC.

17
1806 Jean-Jacques Dessalines, revolutionist and emperor of Haiti, is assassinated in Port-au-Prince.

18
1903 Félix Houphouët-Boigny, president of Ivory Coast, is born in Yamoussoukro.
1926 Rock 'n' roll legend Chuck Berry is born in St. Louis, MO.

19
1878 Dr. Frederick Victor Nanka Bruce, first physician on the Gold Coast, is born in Accra, Ghana.
1936 Dr. Johnnetta Cole, first black female president of Spelman College in Atlanta, GA, is born in Jacksonville, FL.

20
1957 Jomo Kenyatta and five other Mau Mau leaders refuse to appeal their prison terms.

WILLIAM STILL • ABOLITIONIST, WRITER, HISTORIAN

Often called the "Father of the Underground Railroad," William Still (American, 1821–1902) helped hundreds of slaves escape to freedom. He kept careful records of his activities and observations, including brief biographies of the individuals he aided. In 1872 he published these accounts in *The Underground Railroad: A Record of Facts, Authentic Narratives, Letters, &c.,* ... , a remarkable book that recalls the escaping slaves' courage, determination, and ingenuity.

Still was the youngest of eighteen children born to Levin and Charity Still, former slaves who had migrated to New Jersey from the eastern shore of Maryland. At twenty-three Still moved to Pennsylvania, where he became a successful businessman and a founding member and chairman of the Pennsylvania Abolition Society's Vigilance Committee. He also campaigned to end segregation on Philadelphia public transit, established an orphanage for children of African American soldiers and sailors, and founded North Philadelphia's Mission Sabbath School, among other philanthropic acts. Some of Still's writings are in the collection of the Historical Society of Pennsylvania, and his book *The Underground Railroad* is available online at www.gutenberg.org.

Still's community, Lawnside, New Jersey, was an important stop on the Underground Railroad and is now home to the Peter Mott House and Underground Railroad Museum. In 1926 Lawnside was incorporated as a borough, becoming the first independent self-governing African American municipality north of the Mason-Dixon Line.

Wood engraving, artist unknown, 1872

Prints and Photographs Division, LC-USZ62-43634

REV. VONDELL GASSAWAY • FOUNDER, PASTOR OF VERBYCKE SPIRITUAL CHURCH

The Reverend Vondell Verbycke Gassaway of Washington, DC, founded the Verbycke Spiritual Church in 1928 and served as its pastor for thirty-six years. Rev. Gassaway named it for the metaphysical movement in which he was involved, but the renowned photographer who took this image, Gordon Parks, called it St. Martin's. Parks, one of the most creative photographers in history, took this photograph in 1942, at the peak of his career.

In his title for the photograph, Parks describes the pastor "standing in a bowl of sacred water banked with roses, each of which he blesses and gives to a member who has been [anointed] and prayed for by a long line of disciples during the annual 'flower bowl demonstration.'"

Photograph by Gordon Parks
Prints and Photographs Division, LC-DIG-ppmsc-00696

OCTOBER

21 **1872** John H. Conyers Sr. becomes the first African American admitted to the US Naval Academy.

22 **1936** Bobby Seale, cofounder of the Black Panther Party, is born in Dallas, TX.

23 **1886** Wiley Jones opens the first streetcar line in Pine Bluff, AR.

24 **1996** Robert M. Bell becomes the first African American to serve as chief judge of Maryland's court of appeals.

25 **1992** Vivian Dandridge, dancer and singer, dies in Seattle, WA.

26 **1899** Meta Vaux Warrick, African American sculptor, arrives in Paris to meet artist Henry Ossawa Tanner.
        1962 Actor Louise Beavers dies in Los Angeles.

27 **1891** D. B. Downing, inventor, is awarded a patent for the street letter box.
        1924 Actor Ruby Dee is born in Cleveland, OH.

28 **1981** Edward M. McIntyre becomes the first African American mayor of Augusta, GA.

29 **1949** Alonzo G. Moron of the Virgin Islands becomes the first African American president of Hampton Institute, Hampton, VA.

30 **1831** Slave rebellion leader Nat Turner is captured in Virginia.
        1966 Huey Newton and Bobby Seale found the Black Panther Party for Self-Defense in Oakland, CA.

31 **1900** Actor and singer Ethel Waters is born in Chester, PA.

OCTOBER REFLECTIONS

This month I was inspired by:

I'd like to know more about:

The people featured this month and the historical entries brought up these memories:

Next month I would like to:

OCTOBER REFLECTIONS

RANDOM THOUGHTS

BOOKS TO READ

MUSIC TO HEAR

PERFORMANCES TO SEE

NOVEMBER

SUNDAY	MONDAY	TUESDAY	WEDNESDAY	THURSDAY	FRIDAY	SATURDAY
				1	2	3
4	5	6	◑ 7	8	9	10
11	12	● 13	14	15	16	17
18	19	◐ 20	21	22	23	24
25	26	27	○ 28	29	30	

NOV 1   NATIONAL DAY (ANTIGUA)

NOV 3   NATIONAL DAY (DOMINICA)
INDEPENDENCE DAY (PANAMA)

NOV 4   DAYLIGHT SAVING TIME ENDS

NOV 6   ELECTION DAY
GREEN MARCH DAY (MOROCCO)

NOV 11   VETERANS DAY
REMEMBRANCE DAY (CANADA)
INDEPENDENCE DAY (ANGOLA)

NOV 12   VETERANS DAY HOLIDAY

NOV 14   MUHARRAM (BEGINS AT SUNSET)
CHILDREN'S DAY (INDIA)

NOV 18   INDEPENDENCE DAY (MOROCCO)

NOV 19   DISCOVERY DAY (PUERTO RICO)

NOV 22   THANKSGIVING

NOV 24   NATIONAL HOLIDAY (DEMOCRATIC REPUBLIC
OF THE CONGO)
INDEPENDENCE DAY (ZAMBIA)

NOV 25   INDEPENDENCE DAY (SURINAME)

NOV 28   INDEPENDENCE DAY (MAURITANIA)

NOV 30   ST. ANDREW'S DAY (SCOTLAND)
INDEPENDENCE DAY (BENIN)

SUMMIT AVENUE ENSEMBLE

This photograph was taken in the Summit Avenue home and studio of the pioneering African American photographer Thomas E. Askew in Atlanta, Georgia, around 1900. The six young men posing with their musical instruments are, from left, Askew's twin sons, Clarence and Norman Askew, son Arthur Askew, neighbor Jake Sansome, and sons Robert and Walter Askew.

Askew (1850?–1914) was Atlanta's first African American photographer. In his images he portrayed African Americans with pride and dignity. He approached his photography as art, meticulously arranging his subjects' poses while providing soft illumination and thoughtful set backdrops. Thomas Askew told an important story of African American men, women, and children through his portraits.

The full breadth of Askew's legacy has suffered because all of his photographic equipment and negatives were destroyed in the tragic Great Atlanta Fire of 1917.

Photograph by Thomas E. Askew
Prints and Photographs Division, LC-DIG-ppmsca-08772

"above and beyond the call of duty"

DORIE MILLER
*Received the Navy Cross
at Pearl Harbor, May 27, 1942*

ABOVE AND BEYOND THE CALL OF DUTY... ● POSTER BY DAVID STONE MARTIN HONORING DORIE MILLER

It all began on the USS *West Virginia* at Pearl Harbor, Hawaii, early on the morning of December 7, 1941. US Navy Cook Third Class Doris "Dorie" Miller (1919–1943) was collecting laundry when he heard the battle alarm and witnessed the destruction of part of the ship, including his own battle station, and injuries to his shipmates on deck. Miller carried them to safety. With key personnel being taken out, Miller manned an anti-aircraft gun. Without previous training, and without command, he fired at the attacking planes until the ammunition ran out and orders came to abandon the sinking ship.

For his valor Miller received the Navy Cross, at that time the navy's third highest honor. His citation read: "For distinguished devotion to duty, extraordinary courage and disregard for his own personal safety during the attack on the Fleet in Pearl Harbor ... While at the side of his Captain on the bridge, Miller, despite enemy strafing and bombing and in the face of a serious fire, assisted in moving his Captain, who had been mortally wounded, to a place of greater safety, and later manned and operated a machine gun directed at enemy Japanese attacking aircraft until ordered to leave the bridge." Miller was also awarded the Purple Heart; the American Defense Service Medal, Fleet Clasp; the Asiatic Pacific Campaign Medal; and the World War II Victory Medal. In 1973 the US Navy commissioned the USS *Miller* in his honor.

David Stone Martin (American, 1913–1992)
Above and Beyond the Call of Duty—Dorie Miller Received the Navy Cross at Pearl Harbor, May 27, 1942, 1943
Poster
Prints and Photographs Division, LC-USZC4-2328

NOVEMBER

1

1945 John H. Johnson publishes the first issue of *Ebony*.

1999 Chicago Bears Hall of Fame running back Walter "Sweetness" Payton succumbs to liver disease in South Barrington, IL.

2

1983 President Ronald Reagan signs a law designating the third Monday in January as Martin Luther King Jr. Day.

1996 Toni Stone, the first woman to play baseball in the Negro Leagues, dies in Alameda, CA.

3

1983 Jesse Jackson announces his candidacy for the office of president of the United States.

4

1992 Carol Moseley Braun becomes the first African American woman to be elected to the US Senate.

2008 Barack Obama becomes the first African American president of the United States.

5

1862 Frazier A. Boutelle is commissioned as a second lieutenant in the 5th New York Cavalry.

6

1983 Sgt. Farley Simon, a native of Grenada, becomes the first marine to win the Marine Corps Marathon.

1989 Renowned attorney Sadie Tanner Mossell Alexander dies in Philadelphia, PA.

7

1989 Douglas Wilder of Virginia becomes the nation's first black governor since Reconstruction.

8

1938 Crystal Bird Fauset of Pennsylvania becomes the first African American woman to be elected to a state legislature.

9

1731 Benjamin Banneker, scientist and inventor, is born in Ellicott City, MD.

1997 The NBA announces it has hired Dee Kantner and Violet Palmer, the first women to officiate in an all-male major sports league.

10

1917 Musician and writer Nora Holt joins *The Chicago Defender* as the writer of the feature article "Cultivating Symphony Concerts."

1995 Nigerian author and poet Ken Saro-Wiwa is executed in Port Harcourt.

2008 Miriam Makeba, "Empress of African Song," dies in southern Italy.

11   **1989**   The Civil Rights Memorial in Montgomery, AL, is dedicated.

12   **1922**   Sigma Gamma Rho sorority is organized by Mary Lou Allison and six other teachers at Butler University, Indianapolis, IN.

      1941   Lillian Evans Evanti and Mary Cardwell Dawson establish the National Negro Opera Company.

13   **1940**   In *Hansberry v. Lee* the US Supreme Court rules that African Americans cannot be barred from white neighborhoods.

      1998   Kenny Kirkland, jazz pianist with the Branford Marsalis band, dies at his home in Queens, NY.

14   **1954**   Dr. James Joshua Thomas is installed as minister of the Mott Haven Reformed Church in the Bronx, NY.

15   **218 BC**   Hannibal crosses the Alps with 37 elephants and 26,000 men to defeat Roman armies at the Ticino and Trebbia rivers.

      1998   Kwame Ture (Stokely Carmichael) succumbs to prostate cancer in Conakry, Guinea.

16   **1873**   W. C. Handy, "Father of the Blues," is born in Florence, AL.

17   **1911**   Omega Psi Phi fraternity is founded at Howard University.

      1980   WHMM-TV in Washington, DC, becomes the first African American public-broadcasting television station.

18   **1900**   Dr. Howard Thurman, theologian, educator, and civil rights leader, is born in Daytona Beach, FL.

19   **1797**   Abolitionist and women's rights advocate Sojourner Truth is born in Ulster County, NY.

      1997   Drs. Paula Mahone and Karen Drake head a team of 40 specialists in the first successful delivery of septuplets, born in Carlisle, IA.

20   **1695**   Zumbi dos Palmares, Brazilian leader of a 100-year-old rebel slave group, is killed in an ambush.

JULIANN TILLMAN • PREACHER, AME CHURCH

The African Methodist Episcopal (AME) Church, the first independent African American denomination, was established in Pennsylvania in 1816 by the Reverend Richard Allen and colleagues. During the church's early years, as in many denominations, women were not allowed to become pastors. Juliann Jane Tillman sought to overcome sexism within the AME Church and began preaching, contrary to accepted practice and the wishes of her brother and father. Fortunately, Rev. Allen recognized Tillman's calling and approved of her ministry. In this lithograph, which was printed and distributed to reach a broader congregation, Tillman "exhorts the viewer to prepare for the second coming of Christ" by paying close attention to the book of Revelations. Although little is known about Juliann Tillman, it is clear that she was devoted to the AME Church and served tirelessly. Her example inspired other women to ascend to the ministry.

Peter S. Duval (American, b. France, c. 1804–1886)
Mrs. Juliann Jane Tillman, Preacher of the A.M.E. Church, 1844
Lithograph after a painting by Alfred M. Hoffy (American, b. England, 1790–1865)
Prints and Photographs Division, LC-USZC4-4543

AFRICAN AMERICAN TEAMSTERS

In this 1864 Civil War photograph, seven African American teamsters, dressed in old Union uniforms, stand near a signal tower in front of a wagon and shack in the war's main eastern theater at Bermuda Hundred, Virginia. The men were attached to the Army of the James, under the command of Major General Benjamin F. Butler.

It had been common practice not to accept African Americans into military service. When blacks were finally allowed to enlist, in mid-1862, the Union Army often used them as servants, teamsters, and scouts and in other nonmilitary action positions. When they were finally allowed to fight, blacks enlisted in droves to help put an end to slavery. Some 186,000 African American soldiers served in the Union Army, including about 100,000 former slaves.

Bermuda Hundred, Virginia, was named for the colonial practice of measuring land parcels by the "hundreds" (a "hundred" could support one hundred households) and for the British territory of Bermuda, which was once a colony of Virginia.

Photographer unknown
Prints and Photographs Division, LC-DIG-cwpb-02004

NOVEMBER

21
1866 Duse Mohammed Effendi, Egyptian Pan-Africanist, is born.
1893 Granville T. Woods, inventor, patents the electric railway conduit.

22
1994 Jazz musicians Herbie Hancock, Clark Terry, and Joshua Redman perform in a concert beamed by satellite to 60 schools nationwide.

23
1941 Musician and actor Henrietta Vinton Davis dies in Washington, DC.

24
1868 Scott Joplin, composer of ragtime music, is born in Texarkana, TX.

25
1955 The Interstate Commerce Commission bans segregation in interstate travel.

26
1878 Marshall Walter "Major" Taylor, world's fastest bicycle racer for 12 years, is born in Indianapolis, IN.
1927 Marcus Garvey, Pan-Africanist, is released from Tombs Atlanta Penitentiary.

27
1942 Rock musician Jimi Hendrix is born in Seattle, WA.

28
1961 Ernie Davis becomes the first African American to win the Heisman Trophy.

29
1908 Adam Clayton Powell Jr., politician and civil rights activist, is born in New Haven, CT.

30
1912 Gordon Parks, filmmaker and photographer, is born in Fort Scott, KS.

NOVEMBER REFLECTIONS

This month I was inspired by:

I'd like to know more about:

The people featured this month and the historical entries brought up these memories:

Next month I would like to:

NOVEMBER REFLECTIONS

RANDOM THOUGHTS

BOOKS TO READ

MUSIC TO HEAR

PERFORMANCES TO SEE

DECEMBER

SUNDAY	MONDAY	TUESDAY	WEDNESDAY	THURSDAY	FRIDAY	SATURDAY
						1
2	3	4	5	◑ 6	7	8
9	10	11	12	● 13	14	15
16	17	18	19	◑ 20	21	22
23	24	25	26	27	○ 28	29
30	31					

DEC	7	INDEPENDENCE DAY (IVORY COAST)
DEC	8	HANUKKAH (BEGINS AT SUNSET)
DEC	9	INDEPENDENCE DAY (TANZANIA)
DEC	10	HUMAN RIGHTS DAY (GUINEA)
		INDEPENDENCE DAY (PANAMA)
DEC	11	REPUBLIC DAY (BURKINA FASO)

DEC	12	INDEPENDENCE DAY (KENYA)
DEC	18	REPUBLIC DAY (NIGER)
DEC	21	WINTER SOLSTICE 11:12 UTC
DEC	25	CHRISTMAS
		BANK HOLIDAY (CANADA, UK)
DEC	26	BOXING DAY (CANADA, UK)

NEXT OF KIN • LINOCUT BY HELEN JOHANN

During World War II, Detroit was one of a few northern cities to which blacks from the South migrated to find work and a better life. They sought employment by the thousands at automobile manufacturing plants, and this influx raised tensions among white workers who felt they were being pushed out. In 1943 a riot broke out following a fight between black and white youths. The riot lasted three days, and thirty-four people were killed before the National Guard restored order.

This linocut by American artist Helen Johann, depicting an African American woman holding a Detroit newspaper with the headline "Race Riots," was part of the *Artists for Victory* traveling exhibition, which opened at the Metropolitan Museum of Art in New York on December 7, 1942, the first anniversary of the attack on Pearl Harbor. Johann (1901–1990) was one of more than ten thousand artists who joined together to support the country during World War II.

Helen Johann (American, 1901–1990)
Next of Kin
Linocut
Prints and Photographs Division, LC-DIG-ppmsca-19262

STUDENTS AT ATLANTA UNIVERSITY, GEORGIA

These four students, seated on the steps of a building on the Atlanta University campus, represent the future generations of African Americans who would further the progress of their race. The noted Atlanta photographer Thomas E. Askew took this photograph around 1899. It was displayed at the 1900 Paris Exposition Universelle, in an exhibition initiated by W. E. B. Du Bois to show the history and "present conditions" of African Americans. The exhibition included more than five hundred photographs documenting both black progress and the discrimination still prevalent in the United States at the turn of the twentieth century.

Atlanta University, founded in 1865, was the nation's oldest predominantly African American graduate institution. It benefited greatly from the presence of Du Bois, who taught at the university and developed its sociology department. In 1988 the university merged with Clark College to become Clark Atlanta University, which remains a part of the university complex that includes Morris Brown College, Spelman College (exclusively for women), and Morehouse College (exclusively for men).

Photograph by Thomas E. Askew
Prints and Photographs Division, LC-DIG-ppmsca-08778

DECEMBER

1   **1955**   Rosa Parks defies the segregated transportation ordinance in Montgomery, AL, igniting a 382-day bus boycott and launching the civil rights movement in America.

2   **1968**   Dial Press publishes Frank Yerby's *Judas My Brother.*
         2008   Odetta Holmes, folksinger and civil rights activist, dies in New York City.

3   **1911**   Distinguished educator and historian Helen Gray Edmonds is born in Lawrenceville, VA.

4   **1906**   Alpha Phi Alpha fraternity, the first Greek organization for African Americans, is founded at Cornell University.

5   **1870**   Alexandre Dumas (père), French novelist and dramatist, dies in Puys, France.

6   **1960**   Some 500 store owners in Tucson, AZ, sign pledges vowing not to discriminate on the basis of race, color, or religion.
         1997   Lee Brown defeats Rob Mosbacher to become the first black mayor of Houston, TX.

7   **1941**   Dorie Miller, a messman, downs three Japanese planes in the attack on Pearl Harbor.
         1942   Reginald F. Lewis, owner of the first privately held African American Fortune 500 company, is born in Baltimore, MD.

8   **1850**   Lucy Ann Stanton of Cleveland, OH, graduates from Oberlin College with a BA in literature, becoming the first African American woman to complete a four-year college course.
         1987   Kurt Schmoke becomes the first African American mayor of Baltimore, MD.

9   **1919**   Roy DeCarava, the first African American photographer to be awarded a Guggenheim Fellowship, is born in New York City.

10   **1950**   Dr. Ralph J. Bunche becomes the first African American to win the Nobel Peace Prize.

DECEMBER

11   **1920**   Blues singer Willie Mae "Big Mama" Thornton is born in Montgomery, AL.

12   **1995**   Willie Brown defeats incumbent Frank Jordan to become the first African American mayor of San Francisco.

13   **1957**   Daniel A. Chapman becomes Ghana's first ambassador to the United States.
           1998   Former light-heavyweight boxing champion Archie Moore dies in San Diego, CA.

14   **1963**   Dinah Washington, "Queen of the Blues," dies in Detroit, MI.

15   **1883**   William A. Hinton, developer of the Hinton test for diagnosing syphilis, is born in Chicago, IL.

16   **1976**   President Jimmy Carter appoints Andrew Young ambassador to the United Nations.

17   **1760**   Deborah Sampson Gannett, who will disguise herself as a man in order to fight in the Revolutionary War, is born in Plymouth, VA.

18   **1912**   Gen. Benjamin O. Davis Jr. is born in Washington, DC.

19   **1933**   Acclaimed actor Cicely Tyson is born in New York City.

20   **1988**   Max Robinson, first African American news anchor for a major television network, dies in Washington, DC.

J. ROBERT LOVE • PRIEST, PHYSICIAN, AUTHOR

Joseph Robert Love (1839–1914) was born in Nassau, Bahamas, but immigrated in 1866 to the United States, where he was ordained an Episcopal priest in 1876 and attended medical school at the University of Buffalo, graduating in 1879. He may have been the first black at this university to achieve this advanced degree. From 1881 to 1890 he was stationed in Port-au-Prince, Haiti, where he served as a minister and doctor. Roberts eventually left Haiti and settled in Jamaica, where he became a dynamic public speaker, preaching about freedom and religion. Marcus Garvey stated his indebtedness to Love's words.

Dr. Love wrote the book *Romanism Is Not Christianity,* which he distributed to ministers throughout America's South. His ideas centered on the difference between Christianity as taught in the Bible and Christianity as dictated by the Roman elite and the pope. W. E. B. Du Bois was also impressed by Dr. Love and included him in his photographic exhibition of African Americans, displayed at the Exposition Universelle of 1900 in Paris.

Photographer unknown
Prints and Photographs Division, LC-DIG-ppmsca-08841

JOYCE BRYANT • SINGER

Singer Joyce Bryant was known as the Bronze Blond Bombshell for her shapely figure, tight silver gowns, and stylishly coiffed silver-tinted hair. Born in Oakland, California, in 1928, Bryant was raised in San Francisco; in her late teens she moved to Los Angeles, where her singing career began to blossom. She landed a recording contract with Okeh Records, a label known for actively seeking black singers, and began a lucrative career. The poet, playwright, and novelist Carl Hancock Rux wrote, "Known for her amazing four octave voice, stunning beauty, hour-glass figure, [and] provocative outfits, Joyce Bryant was the ultimate show stopper." She is pictured here in 1953.

Unfortunately, for blacks during the 1950s, beauty and a successful career were not without some form of discrimination. For Bryant, being the first black to open at the Aladdin Room of the Algiers Hotel in Miami Beach was ironic because she was not allowed to book a room in that hotel. Continued, often brutal discrimination led to frustration, carelessness, and self-esteem so low that she wasn't able to maintain her status as one of the most impressive entertainers of her day. In 1955 Bryant quit show business and enrolled in Oakwood University, a historically black Seventh-Day Adventist college in Huntsville, Alabama

Photograph by Carl Van Vechten
Prints and Photographs Division, LC-USZ62-92013

DECEMBER

21   **1911**   Josh Gibson, Negro Leagues home run king, is born in Buena Vista, GA.

22   **1883**   Arthur Wergs Mitchell, first African American elected to Congress, is born in Lafayette, AL.
        1898   Chancellor Williams, historian and author of *The Destruction of Black Civilization*, is born in Bennettsville, SC.

23   **1867**   Madame C. J. Walker, first female African American millionaire, is born in Delta, LA.

24   **1853**   Author and teacher Octavia Victoria Rogers Albert is born in Oglethorpe, GA.

25   **1907**   Cab Calloway, bandleader and first jazz singer to sell a million records, is born in Rochester, NY.

26   Kwanzaa begins: Umoja (Unity). *To strive for a principled and harmonious togetherness in the family, community, nation, and world African community.*

27   Kujichagulia (Self-Determination). *To define ourselves, name ourselves, create for ourselves, and speak for ourselves.*

28   Ujima (Collective Work and Responsibility). *To build and maintain our community together; to make our sisters' and brothers' problems our problems and to solve them together.*

29   Ujamaa (Cooperative Economics). *To build our own businesses, control the economics of our own communities, and share in all our communities' work and wealth.*

30   Nia (Purpose). *To make our collective vocation the building and development of our community; to restore our people to their traditional greatness.*

31   Kuumba (Creativity). *To do as much as we can, in whatever way we can, to leave our community more beautiful and beneficial than it was when we inherited it.*

DECEMBER REFLECTIONS

This month I was inspired by:

I'd like to know more about:

The people featured this month and the historical entries brought up these memories:

Next month I would like to:

DECEMBER REFLECTIONS

RANDOM THOUGHTS

BOOKS TO READ

MUSIC TO HEAR

PERFORMANCES TO SEE

2012 INTERNATIONAL HOLIDAYS

Following are the dates of major holidays in 2012 for selected countries. Islamic observances are subject to adjustment. Holidays of the United States, the United Kingdom, and Canada, and major Jewish holidays, appear on this calendar's grid pages. Pomegranate is not responsible for errors or omissions in this list. All dates should be confirmed with local sources before making international travel or business plans.

ARGENTINA
1	Jan	New Year's Day
24	Mar	National Day of Memory for Truth and Justice
2	Apr	Veterans Day (Malvinas War Memorial)
5	Apr	Holy Thursday
6	Apr	Good Friday
8	Apr	Easter
1	May	Labor Day
25	May	First National Government Day
18	Jun	Flag Day
9	Jul	Independence Day
20	Aug	San Martín Day
15	Oct	Día de la Raza
8	Dec	Immaculate Conception
25	Dec	Christmas

AUSTRALIA
1-2	Jan	New Year's Day Holiday
26	Jan	Australia Day
13	Feb	Royal Hobart Regatta (Tas)
5	Mar	Labor Day (WA)
12	Mar	Labor Day (Vic)
		Eight Hours Day (Tas)
		Adelaide Cup (SA)
		Canberra Day (ACT)
6-9	Apr	Easter Holiday
10	Apr	Easter Tuesday (Tas)
25	Apr	ANZAC Day
7	May	May Day (NT)
		Labor Day (Qld)
4	Jun	Foundation Day (WA)
11	Jun	Queen's Birthday (except WA)
		Volunteer's Day (SA)
6	Aug	Picnic Day (NT)
		Bank Holiday (ACT, NSW)
1	Oct	Queen's Birthday (WA)
		Labor Day (ACT, NSW, SA)
8	Oct	Family and Community Day (ACT)
6	Nov	Melbourne Cup (ACT, Vic)
25	Dec	Christmas
26	Dec	Boxing Day (except SA)
		Proclamation Day (SA)

BRAZIL
1	Jan	New Year's Day
20	Jan	São Sebastião Day (Rio de Janeiro)
25	Jan	São Paulo Anniversary (São Paulo)
20-21	Feb	Carnival
22	Feb	Ash Wednesday (until 2 pm)
6	Apr	Good Friday
8	Apr	Easter
21	Apr	Tiradentes Day
1	May	Labor Day
7	Jun	Corpus Christi
7	Sep	Independence Day
12	Oct	Our Lady of Aparecida
2	Nov	All Souls' Day
15	Nov	Proclamation of the Republic
20	Nov	Black Consciousness Day
24	Dec	Christmas Eve (after 2 pm)
25	Dec	Christmas
31	Dec	New Year's Eve (after 2 pm)

CHINA (SEE ALSO HONG KONG)
1-2	Jan	New Year's Day Holiday
22-28	Jan	Spring Festival
4	Apr	Tomb-Sweeping Day
1	May	Labor Day
23	Jun	Dragon Boat Festival
30	Sep	Mid-Autumn Festival
1-3	Oct	National Day Holiday

FRANCE
1	Jan	New Year's Day
8	Apr	Easter
9	Apr	Easter Monday
1	May	Labor Day
8	May	Victory in Europe Day
17	May	Ascension Day
27	May	Pentecost
28	May	Whit Monday
14	Jul	Bastille Day
15	Aug	Assumption
1	Nov	All Saints' Day
11	Nov	Armistice Day
25	Dec	Christmas

GERMANY
1	Jan	New Year's Day
6	Apr	Good Friday
8	Apr	Easter
9	Apr	Easter Monday
1	May	Labor Day
17	May	Ascension Day
27	May	Pentecost
28	May	Whit Monday
3	Oct	Unity Day
25	Dec	Christmas
26	Dec	St. Stephen's Day

HONG KONG
1-2	Jan	New Year's Day Holiday
23-25	Jan	Spring Festival
4	Apr	Tomb-Sweeping Day
6	Apr	Good Friday
7	Apr	Holy Saturday
8	Apr	Easter
9	Apr	Easter Monday
1	May	Labor Day
28	May	Buddha's Birthday
23	Jun	Dragon Boat Festival
1	Jul	Special Administrative Region Establishment Day
30	Sep	Mid-Autumn Festival
1	Oct	National Day
23	Oct	Chung Yeung Festival
25-26	Dec	Christmas Holiday

INDIA
1	Jan	New Year's Day
15	Jan	Makar Sankranti
26	Jan	Republic Day
4	Feb	Milad-un-Nabi
20	Feb	Maha Shivaratri
8	Mar	Holi
1	Apr	Ram Navami
5	Apr	Mahavir Jayanti
6	Apr	Good Friday
8	Apr	Easter
14	Apr	Dr. B. R. Ambedkar's Birthday
6	May	Buddha Purnima
10	Aug	Janmashtami
15	Aug	Independence Day
19	Aug	Ramzan-Eid (Eid-al-Fitr)
2	Oct	Mahatma Gandhi's Birthday
24	Oct	Dussehra (Vijaya Dashami)
26	Oct	Bakr-Eid (Eid-al-Adha)
13	Nov	Diwali (Deepavali)
15	Nov	Islamic New Year
25	Nov	Muharram
28	Nov	Guru Nanak's Birthday
25	Dec	Christmas

IRELAND
1	Jan	New Year's Day
17	Mar	St. Patrick's Day
6	Apr	Good Friday
8	Apr	Easter
9	Apr	Easter Monday
7	May	Bank Holiday
4	Jun	Bank Holiday
6	Aug	Bank Holiday
29	Oct	Bank Holiday
25	Dec	Christmas
26	Dec	St. Stephen's Day

ISRAEL
8	Mar	Purim (except Jerusalem)
9	Mar	Purim Bank Holiday (Jerusalem)
7	Apr	First day of Pesach
14	Apr	Last day of Pesach
19	Apr	Holocaust Memorial Day
25	Apr	National Memorial Day
26	Apr	Independence Day
27	May	Shavuot
29	Jul	Tisha b'Av
17-18	Sep	Rosh Hashanah
26	Sep	Yom Kippur
1	Oct	First day of Sukkot
8	Oct	Shemini Atzeret / Simhat Torah
9	Dec	First day of Hanukkah

ITALY
1	Jan	New Year's Day
6	Jan	Epiphany
8	Apr	Easter
9	Apr	Easter Monday
25	Apr	Liberation Day
1	May	Labor Day

2	Jun	Republic Day
29	Jun	Sts. Peter and Paul (Rome)
15	Aug	Assumption
1	Nov	All Saints' Day
8	Dec	Immaculate Conception
25	Dec	Christmas
26	Dec	St. Stephen's Day

JAPAN

1-2	Jan	New Year's Day Holiday
9	Jan	Coming of Age Day
11	Feb	National Foundation Day
20	Mar	Vernal Equinox
29-30	Apr	Shōwa Day Holiday
3	May	Constitution Memorial Day
4	May	Greenery Day
5	May	Children's Day
16	Jul	Marine Day
17	Sep	Respect for the Aged Day
22	Sep	Autumnal Equinox
8	Oct	Health and Sports Day
3	Nov	Culture Day
23	Nov	Labor Thanksgiving Day
23-24	Dec	Emperor's Birthday Holiday

MEXICO

1	Jan	New Year's Day
6	Feb	Constitution Day
19	Mar	Benito Juárez Day
5	Apr	Holy Thursday
6	Apr	Good Friday
8	Apr	Easter
1	May	Labor Day
17	Sep	Independence Day Holiday
1	Nov	All Saints' Day
2	Nov	All Souls' Day (Day of the Dead)
19	Nov	Revolution Day
1	Dec	Inauguration Day
12	Dec	Our Lady of Guadalupe
25	Dec	Christmas

NETHERLANDS

1	Jan	New Year's Day
6	Apr	Good Friday
8	Apr	Easter
9	Apr	Easter Monday
30	Apr	Queen's Day
17	May	Ascension Day
27	May	Pentecost
28	May	Whit Monday
25-26	Dec	Christmas Holiday

NEW ZEALAND

1-3	Jan	New Year's Holiday
23	Jan	Provincial Anniversary (Wellington)
30	Jan	Provincial Anniversary (Auckland)
6	Feb	Waitangi Day
6	Apr	Good Friday
8	Apr	Easter
9	Apr	Easter Monday
25	Apr	ANZAC Day
4	Jun	Queen's Birthday
22	Oct	Labor Day
16	Nov	Provincial Anniversary (Canterbury)
25	Dec	Christmas
26	Dec	Boxing Day

PUERTO RICO

6	Jan	Three Kings Day (Epiphany)
22	Mar	Emancipation Day
6	Apr	Good Friday
8	Apr	Easter
25	Jul	Constitution Day
8	Oct	Día de la Raza
19	Nov	Discovery of Puerto Rico
24	Dec	Christmas Eve

All US federal holidays also observed

RUSSIA

1-10	Jan	New Year's Holiday
7	Jan	Orthodox Christmas
9	Jan	Orthodox Christmas Holiday
23	Feb	Defenders of the Fatherland Day
8	Mar	International Women's Day
15	Apr	Orthodox Easter
1	May	Spring and Labor Day
9	May	Victory Day
12	Jun	Russia Day
4-5	Nov	National Unity Day Holiday

SINGAPORE

1-2	Jan	New Year's Day Holiday
23-24	Jan	Chinese New Year Holiday
6	Apr	Good Friday
8	Apr	Easter
1	May	Labor Day
5	May	Vesak Day (Buddha's Birthday)
20	Jul	Beginning of Ramadan
9	Aug	National Day
19-20	Aug	Hari Raya Puasa (Eid-al-Fitr) Holiday
26	Oct	Hari Raya Haji (Eid-al-Adha)
13	Nov	Deepavali
25	Dec	Christmas

SOUTH AFRICA

1-2	Jan	New Year's Day Holiday
21	Mar	Human Rights Day
6	Apr	Good Friday
8	Apr	Easter
9	Apr	Family Day
27	Apr	Freedom Day
1	May	Workers' Day
16	Jun	Youth Day
9	Aug	National Women's Day
24	Sep	Heritage Day
16-17	Dec	Day of Reconciliation Holiday
25	Dec	Christmas
26	Dec	Day of Goodwill

SOUTH KOREA

1	Jan	New Year's Day
22-24	Jan	Lunar New Year Holiday
1	Mar	Independence Movement Day
5	May	Children's Day
28	May	Birth of Buddha
6	Jun	Memorial Day
15	Aug	Independence Day
29 Sep-1 Oct		Harvest Moon Festival
3	Oct	National Foundation Day
25	Dec	Christmas

SPAIN

1	Jan	New Year's Day
6	Jan	Epiphany
5	Apr	Holy Thursday
6	Apr	Good Friday
8	Apr	Easter
1	May	Labor Day
15	Aug	Assumption
12	Oct	National Day
1	Nov	All Saints' Day
6	Dec	Constitution Day
8	Dec	Immaculate Conception
25	Dec	Christmas

SWEDEN

1	Jan	New Year's Day
5	Jan	Epiphany Eve
6	Jan	Epiphany
6	Apr	Good Friday
8	Apr	Easter
9	Apr	Easter Monday
30	Apr	Walpurgis Eve
		King's Birthday
1	May	May Day
16	May	Ascension Eve
17	May	Ascension Day
27	May	Pentecost
6	Jun	National Day
22	Jun	Midsummer Eve
23	Jun	Midsummer Day
2	Nov	All Saints' Eve
3	Nov	All Saints' Day
24	Dec	Christmas Eve
25	Dec	Christmas
26	Dec	Boxing Day
31	Dec	New Year's Eve

SWITZERLAND

1	Jan	New Year's Day
6	Apr	Good Friday
8	Apr	Easter
9	Apr	Easter Monday
17	May	Ascension Day
27	May	Pentecost
28	May	Whit Monday
1	Aug	National Day
25	Dec	Christmas
26	Dec	St. Stephen's Day

THAILAND

1-3	Jan	New Year's Day Holiday
7	Mar	Makha Bucha Day
6	Apr	Chakri Day
13-17	Apr	Songkran (Thai New Year)
1	May	Labor Day
5	May	Coronation Day
7	May	Coronation Day Holiday
4	Jun	Visakha Bucha Day (Buddha's Birthday)
2	Aug	Asanha Bucha Day
3	Aug	Khao Phansa (Buddhist Lent begins)
12-13	Aug	Queen's Birthday Holiday
23	Oct	Chulalongkorn Day
28	Nov	Loy Kratong
5	Dec	King's Birthday
10	Dec	Constitution Day
31	Dec	New Year's Eve

WORLD TIME ZONE MAP

This map is based on Coordinated Universal Time (UTC), the worldwide system of civil timekeeping. UTC is essentially equivalent to Greenwich Mean Time. Zone boundaries are approximate and subject to change. Time differences relative to UTC shown here are based on the use of standard time; where Daylight Saving Time (Summer Time) is employed, add one hour to local standard time.

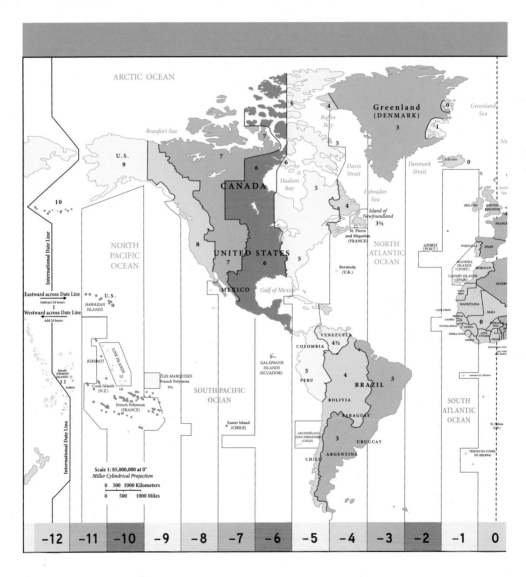

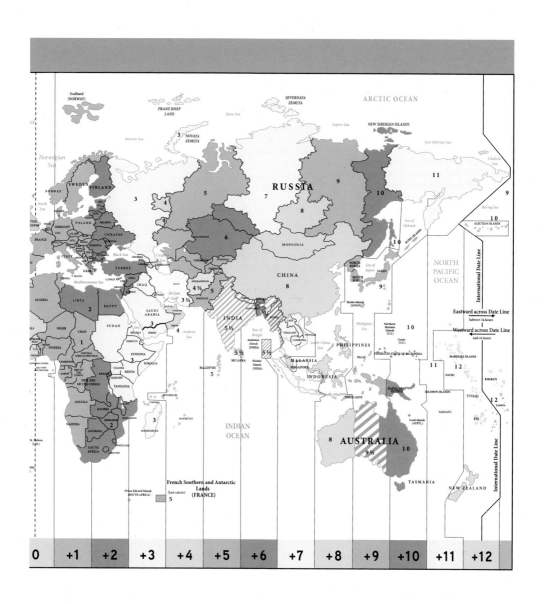

Svalbard
(NORWAY)

FRANZ JOSEF
LAND

SEVERNAYA
ZEMLYA

ARCTIC OCEAN

Kara Sea

Laptev Sea

NEW SIBERIAN ISLANDS

East Siberian Sea

Barents Sea

3 NOVAYA
ZEMLYA

Norwegian
Sea

Chukchi
Sea

11

9

SWEDEN FINLAND

NORWAY

North
Sea

3

4

5

RUSSIA

7

9

10

Bering Sea

ALEUTIAN ISLANDS

10

GERMANY POLAND

FRANCE

UKRAINE

4

KAZAKHSTAN

6

Sea of
Okhotsk

KURILE ISLANDS

Black Sea

GEORGIA

TURKEY

Caspian
Sea

MONGOLIA

NORTH
KOREA

Sea of
Japan

JAPAN

NORTH
PACIFIC
OCEAN

GREECE

CYPRUS

IRAQ

SYRIA

ISRAEL

IRAN

AFGHANISTAN

4½

5

CHINA

8

SOUTH
KOREA

9

Ryuku Islands
(JAPAN)

International Date Line

Mediterranean Sea

MALTA

TUNISIA

JORDAN

Persian
Gulf

3½

PAKISTAN

ALGERIA

LIBYA

2

EGYPT

SAUDI
ARABIA

QATAR

OMAN

4

Arabian
Sea

INDIA

5½

Bay of
Bengal

Andaman
Islands
(INDIA)

LAOS

THAILAND

VIETNAM

CAMBODIA

South China
Sea

Philippine
Sea

PHILIPPINES

Northern
Mariana
Islands
(U.S.)

10

Guam
(U.S.)

Eastward across Date Line

Subtract 24 hours

Westward across Date Line

Add 24 hours

MALI

NIGER

CHAD

1

SUDAN

ERITREA

YEMEN

3

DJIBOUTI

MALDIVES

5

SRI LANKA

5½

Nicobar
Islands
(INDIA)

5½

MALAYSIA

SINGAPORE

PALAU

FEDERATED STATES OF MICRONESIA

MARSHALL ISLANDS

11

12

NAURU

KIRIBATI

BURKINA
FASO

TOGO

NIGERIA

CENTRAL
AFRICAN REPUBLIC

ETHIOPIA

SOMALIA

INDONESIA

11

GHANA

EQUATORIAL GUINEA

SÃO TOMÉ
AND PRINCIPE

CAMEROON

GABON

REP. OF
THE
CONGO

DEM. REP.
OF THE CONGO

UGANDA

KENYA

BURUNDI

RWANDA

International Date Line

SEYCHELLES

TANZANIA

PAPUA NEW
GUINEA

TIMOR LESTE

12

SAMOA

ANGOLA

ZAMBIA

MALAWI

COMOROS

3

MAURITIUS

INDIAN
OCEAN

SOLOMON ISLANDS

TUVALU

12

FIJI

NAMIBIA

ZIMBABWE

2

MADAGASCAR

VANUATU

St. Helena
(U.K.)

BOTSWANA

MOZAMBIQUE

Coral Islands
(AUSTL.)

8

AUSTRALIA

SOUTH
AFRICA

SWAZILAND

LESOTHO

9½

10

Prince Edward Islands
(SOUTH AFRICA)

French Southern and Antarctic
Lands
(FRANCE)

ÎLES CRAOZET

5

ÎLES KERGUELEN

TASMANIA

NEW ZEALAND

| 0 | +1 | +2 | +3 | +4 | +5 | +6 | +7 | +8 | +9 | +10 | +11 | +12 |

2013

JANUARY

s	m	t	w	t	f	s
		1	2	3	4	5
6	7	8	9	10	11	12
13	14	15	16	17	18	19
20	21	22	23	24	25	26
27	28	29	30	31		

FEBRUARY

s	m	t	w	t	f	s
					1	2
3	4	5	6	7	8	9
10	11	12	13	14	15	16
17	18	19	20	21	22	23
24	25	26	27	28		

MARCH

s	m	t	w	t	f	s
					1	2
3	4	5	6	7	8	9
10	11	12	13	14	15	16
17	18	19	20	21	22	23
24	25	26	27	28	29	30
31						

APRIL

s	m	t	w	t	f	s
	1	2	3	4	5	6
7	8	9	10	11	12	13
14	15	16	17	18	19	20
21	22	23	24	25	26	27
28	29	30				

MAY

s	m	t	w	t	f	s
			1	2	3	4
5	6	7	8	9	10	11
12	13	14	15	16	17	18
19	20	21	22	23	24	25
26	27	28	29	30	31	

JUNE

s	m	t	w	t	f	s
						1
2	3	4	5	6	7	8
9	10	11	12	13	14	15
16	17	18	19	20	21	22
23	24	25	26	27	28	29
30						

JULY

s	m	t	w	t	f	s
	1	2	3	4	5	6
7	8	9	10	11	12	13
14	15	16	17	18	19	20
21	22	23	24	25	26	27
28	29	30	31			

AUGUST

s	m	t	w	t	f	s
				1	2	3
4	5	6	7	8	9	10
11	12	13	14	15	16	17
18	19	20	21	22	23	24
25	26	27	28	29	30	31

SEPTEMBER

s	m	t	w	t	f	s
1	2	3	4	5	6	7
8	9	10	11	12	13	14
15	16	17	18	19	20	21
22	23	24	25	26	27	28
29	30					

OCTOBER

s	m	t	w	t	f	s
		1	2	3	4	5
6	7	8	9	10	11	12
13	14	15	16	17	18	19
20	21	22	23	24	25	26
27	28	29	30	31		

NOVEMBER

s	m	t	w	t	f	s
					1	2
3	4	5	6	7	8	9
10	11	12	13	14	15	16
17	18	19	20	21	22	23
24	25	26	27	28	29	30

DECEMBER

s	m	t	w	t	f	s
1	2	3	4	5	6	7
8	9	10	11	12	13	14
15	16	17	18	19	20	21
22	23	24	25	26	27	28
29	30	31				